Your Library Goes Virtual

Audrey P. Church

Professional Development Resources for K-12
Library Media and Technology Specialists

Copyright

Chesterfield County Public Schools (CCPS) OPAC homepage screenshots reprinted with permission from The Library Corporation.

Springfield Township High School Library homepage screenshots reprinted with permission from Joyce Valenza, Library Media Specialist, Springfield Township High School.

Walter Reed Middle School Library homepage screenshots reprinted with permission from Mark Bobrosky, Library Media Teacher, Walter Reed Middle School.

Paideia School Library homepage screenshots reprinted with permission from Natalie Bernstein, Elementary Librarian, Paideia School.

KidsClick! Worlds of Web Searching page screenshots reprinted with permission from Jerry Kuntz, Electronic Resources Consultant, Ramapo Catskill Library System.

Research Rocket tutorial from the Elementary/Kids section of the Kentucky Virtual Library screenshots reprinted with permission from Enid Wohlstein, Director, Kentucky Virtual Library, a unit of Kentucky Virtual University, at the Kentucky Council on Postsecondary Education.

John Newbery Elementary Library Media Center homepage screenshots reprinted with permission from Jeanne Barnes, Teacher-Librarian, John Newbery Elementary.

Greece Athena Media Center homepage screenshots reprinted with permission from Will Haines, Librarian, Greece Athena Middle School.

MAGNOLIA homepage screenshots reprinted with permission from Stephen Cunetto, Administrator of Systems, Mississippi State University Libraries.

MARVEL homepage screenshots reprinted with permission from Bonnie Dwyer, Central Maine Library District Consultant, Maine State Library.

BadgerLink homepage screenshots reprinted with permission from James Leaver, BadgerLink Coordinator, Department of Public Instruction.

Electronic Library for Minnesota (ELM) homepage screenshots reprinted with permission from Mary Parker, Associate Director, MINITEX Library Information Network.

ODLIS definition of "pathfinder" reprinted with permission from Joan Reitz.

Definition of "WebQuest" reprinted with permission from Bernie Dodge, Ph.D., Professor of Educational Technology, San Diego State University.

Excerpts of blog entries from December 30, 2005, Teens and Virtual Libraries, reprinted with permission from Joyce Valenza.

Excerpts of blog entries from January 4, 2006, Interface Creep, reprinted with permission from Joyce Valenza.

Library of Congress Cataloging-in-Publication Data

Church, Audrey P., 1957-
  Your library goes virtual / Audrey P. Church.
      p. cm.
      Includes bibliographical references and index.
      ISBN 1-58683-219-0 (pbk.)
 1. School libraries—Information technology. 2. Library Web sites. 3. Internet in school libraries. 4. Digital libraries. 5. Libraries—Special collections—Computer network resources. I. Title.

Z675.S3C53 2007
025.04—dc22
              2006025776

Cynthia Anderson: Acquisitions Editor
Carol Simpson: Editorial Director
Judi Repman: Consulting Editor

Published by Linworth Publishing, Inc.
480 East Wilson Bridge Road, Suite L
Worthington, Ohio 43085

Copyright © 2007 by Linworth Publishing, Inc.

All rights reserved. No part of this book may be electronically reproduced, transmitted, or recorded without written permission from the publisher.

ISBN: 1-58683-219-0

Table of Contents

Table of Figures	7
Acknowledgments/About the Author	9
Introduction	11
Chapter 1: Why Go Virtual? What the Research Tells Us	**13**
Where are the students?	15
From what location do the students go online?	16
What of our younger children?	18
How do students find what they need on the Internet? Are they successful?	19
Where do school libraries fit?	20
Where do teachers fit?	21
What do students want, in general?	22
What does this research mean for virtual school libraries?	23
What features should we include, if we pay attention to students?	23
What should we know as we develop virtual school libraries?	24
Conclusion	25
Chapter 2: Information Access and Delivery: The Information Content of the Virtual Library	**27**
Online Catalog	28
Subscription Databases	30
General Periodical Databases	32
General Encyclopedia Databases	33
Subject Area Specialized Databases	33
Reference Access	34
Professional Collection	35
Professional ebooks	36
Journal Access for Professional Development	37
Parents' Space	37
Ebooks (Fee and Free)	38

Web Site Subscriptions	39
Locally Selected Web Sites	40
Sample Dictionary Sites	40
Sample Ready Reference Sites	41
Sample Biographical Links	41
Sample Geographical Links	42
Sample Government Sites, Federal	42
Federated or Meta Searching	43
Access from within *Blackboard*	44
Conclusion	45
Exemplary Web Pages for Information Access and Delivery	46

Chapter 3: Learning and Teaching: What It Is All About — 49

Curriculum Support	51
Pathfinders	51
WebQuests	52
Information Literacy Skills Instruction	53
Basic Instruction in Information Literacy	53
Effective Use of Search Tools	54
Evaluating Web Sites	55
The Research Process: Research Guides	56
Citations and Ethical Use of Information	57
Reading Promotion	59
Virtual Librarian Services	60
Conclusion	61
Exemplary Web Pages for Learning and Teaching	62

Chapter 4: Program Administration: Steps to Implementing a Virtual Library — 65

Needs Analysis for Virtual Content and Services	66
Collection Development Considerations	68
Attention to Policies	69
District Policies Related to Web Page Content	69
District Policies Related to Web Page Services	70
Library Policies Regarding Virtual Reference Service	71

    Training   73
    Workload   75
    Marketing for the Virtual Library   75
        On-Paper Possibilities   76
        In-Person Possibilities   77
        Promotional Item Possibilities   77
        Virtual Possibilities   78
    Evaluation of the Virtual Library   79
    Evaluation Criteria   79
    Feedback from Users   80
    Conclusion   82

Chapter 5: Technological Aspects   83
    Larger School Technology Context   84
    Web Design   85
        Planning   85
        Layout and Appearance   86
        Usability   87
        Readability   89
        Accessibility Issues   89
        Testing, Upkeep, and Maintenance   91
    Conclusion   92

Chapter 6: The Larger Learning Community: Where Are We Now?   93
    School Library Media Center Web Pages: 1996-2006   94
    State-Level Virtual Libraries Providing Services for K-12 Schools   96
    Virtual Libraries Serving Virtual K-12 Schools   102
    Virtual Libraries: Present and Future   103

List of Sites Mentioned   107

Works Cited   113

Index   119

Table of Figures

Figure 2.1
  Chesterfield County Public Schools TLC OPAC homepage   29

Figure 2.2
  Greece Athena Media Center homepage   46

Figure 2.3
  Walter Reed Middle School Library homepage   47

Figure 2.4
  Paideia School Library homepage   48

Figure 3.1
  KidsClick! Worlds of Web Searching homepage   53

Figure 3.2
  Kentucky Virtual Library Research Rocket
     Tutorial homepage   57

Figure 3.3
  John Newbery Elementary Library homepage   62

Figure 3.4
  Springfield Township High School Library homepage   63

Table 6.1
  State Virtual Library URLs   97

Figure 6.2
  MAGNOLIA K-12 homepage   98

Figure 6.3
  MARVEL! homepage   99

Figure 6.4
  BadgerLink homepage   100

Figure 6.5
  ELM homepage   100

Table 7.1
  List of Sites Mentioned   107

Acknowledgments

The author wishes to acknowledge the following for their assistance with this book:

> Thanks to Cyndee Anderson, Acquisitions Editor, for convincing me that I really did have the time to write this one.
>
> Thanks to Sherry York, Project Editor, for her patience, her kind diplomacy, and her gracious guidance.
>
> Thanks to those who reviewed the manuscript, for their positive comments and constructive suggestions.
>
> This book is dedicated to my family, without whose support I would never be able to write, and to you, the reader, for whom the book was truly written.

Note: At the time of publication, all URLs presented were valid links.

About the Author

Audrey Puckett Church was a building level library media specialist in Virginia public schools for 20 years. Currently she coordinates and teaches in the graduate program in school library media at Longwood University in Farmville, Virginia. A frequent presenter at regional, state, and national conferences, she is past president of her state professional organization, the Virginia Educational Media Association, and past secretary of the Educators of Library Media Specialists Section of the American Association of School Librarians. Her first book, *Leverage Your Library Program to Help Raise Test Scores: A Guide for Library Media Specialists, Principals, Teachers, and Parents,* was published by Linworth in 2003. In *Your Library Goes Virtual,* she offers guidance for creating a school library presence on the Web.

Introduction

This book is written as a user-friendly, practical guide to assist school library media specialists in providing a quality virtual presence for their libraries. Twenty plus years ago, I became a library media specialist because I love libraries and I love books, and I do not believe that electronic/digital/virtual can ever replace a physical library or that an ebook can actually replace a book that I can hold in my hands. Any school library today that intends to serve its patrons effectively and efficiently and to help them to become independent, information literate, lifelong learners, however, *must* have a virtual presence.

The technology survey reported in the June 2005 *School Library Journal* showed that two-thirds of school libraries now have library Web pages (Brewer and Milam 51). One only has to go to Peter Milbury's *School-Libraries.net* Web site to find examples for all grade levels from all over the world. As we look at school library media center Web sites, however, content and quality vary greatly. Many Web pages still offer only library hours, names of library staff, and library policies and procedures. This book is for library media specialists whose pages I have just described. It will provide you with an overview of what you might include on your revitalized Web page to better represent your library to the world and make it the learning tool that it should be for your students. For those whose Web pages go beyond what I described, this book is for you also. As you read, perhaps you will find ideas that you had not thought of, items that you had not considered including, or new ways of presenting content and information.

As instructor in the graduate program in school library media at Longwood University, I frequently teach both Informational Sources and Services (our reference course) and Collaborative Instructional Processes (our collaboration course). Occasionally, I teach our Production of Media for Instruction course, in which students construct Web pages for their school libraries. As I have taught these courses, the pieces for this book have come together: I am convinced that school libraries play a major role in student learning, that more and more learning and interaction will occur online, and that if we do not want our libraries to be left behind, we have to develop that virtual library presence.

The purpose of this book is to serve as a "thought-provoker" and a guide for those exploring the concept of virtual school libraries or working to develop one. It is written to assist you as you build or revamp a school library media center Web page to make it a virtual school library. It is intended for building-level and district-level library media specialists, for school administrators desiring to better understand library service in today's information environment, for technology coordinators/directors, and, perhaps, for graduate students in school library media programs who are pondering the Web presence of their libraries.

Your Library Goes Virtual is structured using the key concepts from *Information Power: Building Partnerships for Learning*. Chapter 1 reviews and summarizes current research regarding student and teacher use of electronic resources and discusses the implications of these research findings in the context of the development of the school library media center Web page. Chapter 2 addresses Information Access and Delivery, the information content of the library Web page, and Chapter 3 addresses Learning and Teaching, the instructional component of the library Web page. In Chapter 4, we look at Program Administration and what is involved in the effective development and implementation of the Web page, while in Chapter 5 we examine the technological aspects to be considered. Chapter 6 explores school library Web pages in the context of the larger learning community. Features of exemplary school library Web sites are highlighted throughout the book. Works cited, a list of Web sites mentioned in the book, and an index complete the work.

CHAPTER ONE

Why Go Virtual?
What the Research Tells Us

Flashback: 1986—Sarah has a research paper to write for her ninth grade earth science class, and she has chosen the planet Saturn as her topic. Her teacher has taken the class to the library three days during fourth period, and Sarah has taken notes from an encyclopedia, checked out two books on the planet, and copied citations for three journal articles from the green and gold *Reader's Guide to Periodical Literature.* She is to stop by the library after sixth period to pick up the magazines for overnight checkout, but she forgets to stop by the library and she forgets to retrieve the books from her locker, and her paper is due tomorrow.

Flash forward: 2006—Sarah has a research paper to write for her ninth grade earth science class, and she has chosen the planet Saturn as her topic. Using the pathfinder created by the library media specialist in collaboration with her earth science teacher and loaded on the library media center Web page, Sarah has searched the online catalog using the suggested subject headings and found two books on her planet, one of which is an ebook. She has accessed and taken notes from the science database to which the library subscribes. She has also pulled several full-text journal articles from the periodical database and visited a couple of the Web sites suggested in the pathfinder. She has checked out the one physical book from the library, and she is confident that she has enough relevant, up-to-date information to write her research paper. If she finds any gaps tonight as she is writing her paper, she will just go online, access the school library media center's Web page, and work from there to find what she needs.

The difference? Twenty years and technology . . . different resource formats, different library services, and a different type of patron. As noted by the *Beloit College Mindset List for the Class of 2009*, freshmen born in 1987 and entering college in the fall of 2005 "don't remember when 'cut and paste' involved scissors . . . learned to count with Lotus 1-2-3 . . . may have fallen asleep playing with their Gameboys in the crib . . . [and live in a world in which] digital cameras have always existed" (Neif 2-5). Students currently enrolled in our K-12 schools have grown up in similar, if not more technologically advanced, environments. Children of today are different; they learn differently, and they think differently than did children of 20, 15, even 10 years ago. They have grown up with video, cable TV, cell phones, video games, digital technology, and the Internet. They are not afraid of technology, and they learn, actively, by doing.

In his eye-opening work published in 1998, *Growing Up Digital: The Rise of the Net Generation*, Don Tapscott discusses how the Net Generation, those raised with digital technology and the Internet as an integral part of their lives, think, communicate, learn, play, and work differently than do earlier generations. In the chapter examining N-Gen Learning, he points out that we now live in a knowledge-based economy, and he insists on a new model of learning, one that is participatory, constructivist, interactive, discovery-based, and that requires critical thinking (127). Only when we in education accept this paradigm shift and adjust our teaching accordingly will we provide effective instruction for today's N-Gen learners.

Likewise, "today's school libraries have become far more than simple repositories of books" or collections of resources (*School Library* 1). "Libraries and digital information resources can play a critical role in the education of today's students" (Lippincott 13.1) as we "provide collections, organized information, systems that promote access, and in-person and virtual assistance to encourage students to pursue their education beyond the classroom" (Lippincott 13.2). As David Warlick notes in his *Knowledge Quest* article, "Building Web Sites That Work for Your Media Center," as library media specialists "we must challenge ourselves to step back and examine the overarching goals of our job—assisting students to become successful learners as well as supporting teachers in their efforts to create and craft meaningful learning experiences for their students—and to do this within the context of a contemporary information environment" (13).

As Ross Todd so aptly states, we must rethink and expand the concept of "school library" from "not just an information place but also as a knowledge space" (6). Our library becomes not only physical space within four walls but also information access and information literacy instruction provided at the point and place of student need. David Loertscher asserts the library is Network Central, centralized and decentralized simultaneously, meeting student needs whenever and wherever they occur (6). To do this in today's digital environment, our libraries must have virtual presence, accomplished through an effective school library media center Web page, providing "online services 24 hours a day, seven days a week" (Loertscher and Achterman 6).

In this chapter we will examine some of the key research concerning students' information needs and patterns of technology usage, take a look at some current library statistics, and fit it all into the context of providing virtual library service for our students. As noted in the Yahoo-conducted 2003 *Born to be Wired* study, "to reach them, [we] must go where they are" (27).

Where are the students?

We look to surveys conducted by the Pew Internet and American Life Project and by Yahoo for answers. To say that today's youth use the Internet would be putting it mildly. According to a November 2004 Pew Internet and American Life Project survey, "the number of teenagers using the Internet has grown 24% in the past four years and 87% of those between the ages of 12 and 17 are online . . . About 21 million teens use the Internet and half of them say they go online every day" (*Teens Forge* 1).

Students note that they use the Internet as a virtual textbook and reference library, as a virtual tutor and study shortcut, a virtual study group, a virtual guidance counselor, and a virtual locker, backpack, and notebook. "Internet-savvy students rely on the Internet to help them to do their school work . . . Virtually all use the Internet to do research to help them write papers or complete class work or homework assignments" (*Digital Disconnect* ii). Students consider the

Internet as "virtual textbook and reference library. Much like a school-issued textbook or traditional library, students think of the Internet as the place to find primary and secondary source material for their reports, presentations, and projects" (*Digital Disconnect* iii).

When asked why they prefer the Internet, students say the Internet is easier to use and more convenient than traditional libraries, does not require transportation to and from, is open 24/7, has up-to-date material, is "always available to everyone (as distinct from a library book that might be checked out by a classmate)" (*Digital Disconnect* 8). Additional areas in which the Internet wins out over traditional libraries: Libraries offer limited selections of multimedia and require students to wait in line to check out materials and to pay to use the copier.

Findings from *Born to be Wired* echo those from the Pew Internet and American Life Project surveys. According to *Born to be Wired*, "the Internet has become THE youth medium of choice . . . time spent with the Internet now exceeds the time spent with television for the "Millennial" generation, youths aged 13 to 24" (ii). Sixty-five percent of youth ages 13-18 noted that it was important that Web sites give you a place to do research (*Born* 24) and Lippincott, in *Educating the Net Generation: Net Generation Students and Libraries,* states that "Net Gen students clearly perceive the open space of the World Wide Web as their information universe" (13.3).

> **Implications**
>
> Students are online; they use the Internet for research for schoolwork, homework assignments, and research papers. We need to provide school library media center Web pages that are easy to use, are available 24/7, and provide up-to-date resources and materials. Students are online, and our library resources and services should be there also.

From what location do the students go online?

We look to the National Council for Education Statistics and the Pew Internet and American Life Project for answers. According to the National Center for Education Statistics, "in fall 2002, 99 percent of public schools in the United States had access to the Internet" (*Internet* 1), this up from 89 percent in 1998 and 35 percent in 1994. Certainly today's youth have Internet access from their schools. Interestingly, though, according to the Pew Internet and American Life 2002 study, *The Digital Disconnect*, "for the most part, students' educational use of the Internet occurs outside of the school day, outside of the school building, outside the direction of their teachers" (iii). Students attribute much of this outside use of the Internet to administrative policies regarding Internet use within school, teacher policies regarding Internet use in and for class, quality of access to the Internet within the school building, and filtering software that blocks legitimate educational use sites (*Digital Disconnect* iii-iv).

The July 2005 *Teens Forge Forward* study affirms this use outside of school: "Teens, too, are accessing the Internet from a variety of locations, including their homes (87%), schools (78%), community centers (9%), libraries (54%), and friends' and relatives' houses (74%)" (2). Seventy-six percent of online teens who go online from more than one place go online most from home (*Teens Technology* 6).

"Just 13% of teens who connect to the Web from school do not also have Web access at their home. These teens tend to be online much less often than all online teens who have access from home *and* school. Twenty-eight percent of teens who go online at home and school report going online several times a day and 28% go online about once a day. Of the teens who go online at school and not from home, only 7% say they go online several times a day and 15% say they go online about once a day. While school can be a location that allows teens to get access to the Web when they do not have access as readily elsewhere, those teens with online access at home are able to go online much more frequently" (*Teens Technology* 2).

Joyce Valenza, in her current doctoral research, examines similar questions. Reporting on early analysis of her data (looking at student use of 14 high school library Web sites identified as those that illustrate best practice), she finds that "at four of the 14 schools, well over 60% of the students report using the site when they are not at school. At seven of the schools, less than 40% report using the site when not at school" (*Interface*). While weekend use was low, "in only two schools was the level of use around or more than 50%," "students at six of the schools report evening use at around 50% or higher" (*Interface*).

> **Implications**
>
> Students go online from various locations, many outside of the school environment. As might be expected, students with access from home are online more frequently than those who are only online at school. Students use library Web sites from home, some on the weekends, but more in the evenings. Library Web pages provide 24/7 access to resources. Truly, we must reach out to students where they are.

What of our younger children?

Again, the National Center for Education Statistics and the Pew Internet and American Life Project provide answers. According to the National Center for Education Statistics, in 2000 "almost all young children [kindergarteners and first graders] had access to computers, either at home or in their classrooms and schools" (*Young* ix). "Classroom Internet use for young children was not prevalent" (*Young* xi). "Public school children's access to computer resources at school and home tended to increase as they moved from kindergarten to first grade" (*Young* xiii).

Recent federal legislation may increase access to computers and the Internet for elementary age children. "As part of the No Child Left Behind Act of 2001 (NCLB, P. L. 107-110), the Enhancing Education Through Technology (ED Tech) program seeks to improve achievement in elementary and secondary schools through the use of technology, to assist students to become technically literate by the eighth grade, and to ensure that teachers integrate technology into the curriculum to improve student achievement. There are also provisions in the act to provide funding for schools to purchase technology resources to further the program's goals" (*Young* v).

In fact, fast forward to 2005: "One-quarter of teenagers agreed that if a child is not using the Internet by the time they start school, they will fall behind their peers while 44% of parents believed the same thing. While most parents and teens view the Internet as a helpful academic tool, parents are more likely to believe that children must be familiar with the Web by the time they start school" (*Teens Technology* 3).

> **Implications**
>
> It is important for not only high schools and middle schools but also elementary schools to provide virtual library services via the school library Web page. Guided access to appropriate information on the free Internet and in subscription databases as well as early information literacy instruction is valuable for our younger students.

How do students find what they need on the Internet? Are they successful?

Lippincott in *Educating the Net Generation: Net Generation Students and Libraries,* reports that "one study at Colorado State University yielded information that 58 percent of freshmen used Google or a comparable search engine first, while only 23 percent started with a database or index" (13.4). When given a research assignment, students go to search tools first. How effective are the students at searching the Internet? What do they find?

A January 2005 Pew Internet report, *Search Engine Users*, found that 97% of Internet users under 30 years express confidence in their search skills" and "72% of Internet users under 30 years say search engines are fair and unbiased" (iv). Additionally, "68% of users say that search engines are a fair and unbiased source of information" (*Search Engine* i). "62% of searchers are not aware of a distinction between paid and unpaid results" (*Search Engine* ii).

According to *The Digital Disconnect*, "the single greatest irritation facing students is their use of search engines that point them to online information that is not trustworthy or understandable to them" (8). They note that "search engines regularly retrieve too many references for common Internet searches. Authorship of Web sites and timeliness of posted information is often not disclosed; the information on many Web sites can be biased or incomplete; and, the reading level of the best information may exceed the capabilities and comprehension of students" (24).

Lippincott asserts, "while many of today's Net Gen students have grown up with technology, they do not necessarily have the requisite knowledge or skills to use technology and digital information in ways appropriate to the academy" (13.5). She also reports that "while students rated themselves highly in their ability to find information on the Internet, they recognized that they floundered when they attempted to find materials appropriate for their research and wasted much time in the process" (13.7).

> ### Implications
> Students tend to begin their research with a general search tool. They need assistance in effectively using search tools, in understanding the results retrieved, and in evaluating the information found. They also need to learn that a search tool may not be the best place to start their research process.

Where do school libraries fit?

The National Center for Education Statistics surveyed school librarians and 15,000-plus tenth graders in more than 750 schools and reported their findings in *School Library Media Centers: Selected Results from the Education Longitudinal Study of 2002 (ELS: 2002)*. Librarians were asked about collections, services, and collaboration, and "students were asked how often they used the school library for different purposes, and their opinions about library resources and staff" (2).

"Of the database services that *ELS:2002* asked school librarians about, 88 percent of school libraries had reference/bibliography databases, 82 percent had general articles and news databases, 62 percent had college and career databases, and 56 percent had academic subject databases" (iv). School libraries, therefore, offer subscription databases for their patrons' use; there is no lack of quality information available.

"The majority of students found their school library reference materials useful. Fifty-eight percent reported the reference materials in their school library were useful, and another 22 percent found their school library reference materials very useful" (16). "Well over half of students reported that library staff was helpful with several tasks. Seventy-nine percent of students reported that the library staff was very helpful or helpful with finding research resources. Sixty-five percent of students reported that the library staff was very helpful or helpful with using databases. Sixty-nine percent of students reported that the library staff was very helpful or helpful with using the Internet" (16).

"Students reported using the school library sometimes or often for research papers (54 percent), in-school projects (53 percent), Internet access (41 percent), and assignments (41 percent)" (14). Interestingly, too, data analysis showed that "students with higher test scores were more likely than students with lower test scores to use the library sometimes or often for assignments, in-school projects, and research papers" (15). Findings from Ross Todd and Carol Kuhlthau's Ohio study echo the *ELS:2002* report. "Effective school libraries in Ohio are dynamic rather than passive agents of learning . . . the effective school library helps the strongest as a resource agent and a technical agent, providing access to information resources necessary for students to complete their research assignments and projects successfully . . . provides access to both print collections within the library and electronic resources through databases and the World Wide Web" (4-5).

The effective school library functions as "not just an information place but also as a knowledge space where students develop the appropriate information literacy scaffolds to enable them to engage with information and build new knowledge. An effective school library is not just informational, but formational" (6).

Implications

Students find library staff and library resources helpful and note that they positively impact their learning; we must translate this helpfulness into the virtual environment, and we must include not only access to information but also instruction in how to evaluate and to use that information.

Where do teachers fit?

According to the NCES *Teachers' Tools for the 21st Century: A Report on Teachers' Use of Technology* published in 2000, which examined teachers' instructional use of computers and the Internet, "nearly all public school teachers (99 percent) reported having computers available somewhere in their schools in 1999" (ii). Fifty-one percent of these teachers assigned Internet research (i). "Teachers who spent more time in professional development activities were generally more likely than teachers who spent less time in such activities to indicate they felt well prepared or very well prepared to use computers and the Internet for instruction" (iv).

Williams, Grimble, and Irwin conducted an exploratory study at an Indiana high school to investigate "teachers' awareness of electronic resources and to determine whether their directions influence student use of these resources in the SLMC. . . . Findings revealed that teachers encourage student Internet use in the SLMC, but most do not direct students to use databases. Teachers consider information from electronic databases to be more reliable and focused, but they say the Internet is faster, easier to use, and has a greater scope of information" (1). The library impact studies conducted by Keith Curry Lance and his associates demonstrate that library media specialists should provide in-service and professional development in the area of information technology for teachers (Lance, Rodney, Hamilton-Pennell 7). Teachers should be aware of and trained in the use of subscription databases and other library information resources.

> **Implications**
>
> More and more teachers are using the Internet for instruction and assigning research projects, which require use of the Internet and other electronic resources. We need to provide training for teachers in the use of available information technologies, and we need to collaborate with teachers to make sure that student research is as effective and productive as possible.

What do students want, in general?

According to *The Digital Disconnect* study, " . . . students have an increasingly new set of needs and expectations for learning that are based on using the Internet. These students said over and over again that their schools and teachers have not yet recognized—much less responded to—the fundamental shift occurring in the students they serve and in the learning communities they are charged with fostering" (5). "Students maintain that schools should place priority on developing programs to teach keyboarding, computer, and Internet literacy skills" (v) and " . . . want better coordination of their out-of-school educational use of the Internet with classroom activities. They argue that this could be the key to leveraging the power of the Internet for learning" (iv).

The *Born to be Wired* study reports that "this generation has had a very structured upbringing, and they're seeking more structure online. They demand efficiency.... They seek structure not because they want to be told what to do, but because they've got a lot to do online, and simply don't want to waste time" (iii). It also notes that "the online world is seen as vast and limitless to young people, but it can also be frustrating if they appear directionless and inefficient. They are truly searching for sites and advertisers to erect signposts and on-ramps on the information superhighway, and to help make their online experiences more efficient" (23). "Students urge that there should be continued effort to ensure that high-quality online information to complete school assignments be freely available, easily accessible, and age-appropriate— without undue limitation on students' freedom" (*Digital Disconnect* v).

What does this research mean for virtual school libraries?

"As Tony Comper, president of the Bank of Montreal, says: 'Kids doing a random walk through all the information in the world is not necessarily the best way for them to learn. Teachers [library media specialists] can become navigators providing meta-learning—crucial guidance and support regarding how to go about learning.' Professor Owston at York University in Toronto agrees: 'We do have to make sure that the engagement with the Internet is stimulating and intelligent. We must remember that it's not the Internet itself that will do that— it's the teacher [library media specialist] who mediates the students' engagement with the Internet'" (Tapscott 154).

In his book, *Redefining Literacy for the 21st Century,* David Warlick discusses literacy, information, and learning, noting that children "need to learn to control their information in positive, productive, and personally meaningful ways—and this is what we need to be teaching them" (22). We, as library media specialists, are information mediators and information guides. Virtual school libraries are "... a step in the right direction, taking library resources to where students want to find them" (Lippincott 13.4).

What features should we include, if we pay attention to students?

As Lee Rainie reported in his October 2005 *Internet Librarians* speech, "Teens are using IM and those [cell] phones to redefine the very notion of what it means to be 'present' with other people. Physical proximity matters less and less. So does the time of day. So does the venue . . . we need to re-think our ideas of what it means to 'be with' others" (4). "The vision of technologists that is becoming a reality for more and more Internet users is that they can access each other and information anytime, anywhere, on a variety of devices" (8). If our libraries are to provide needed services, we must embrace the concept of virtual; time and geographical place are less relevant than ever before.

Another concept that Rainie shares in his speech, which has implications for Web page development, is that of former Microsoft executive Linda Stone's—*continuous partial attention*: "Continuous partial attention is not the same as multitasking; that's about trying to accomplish several things at once. With continuous partial attention, we're scanning incoming alerts for the one best thing to seize upon: 'How can I tune in in a way that helps me sync up with the most interesting or important opportunity?'" (10). Our students will function in the mode of continuous partial attention, scanning for elements or information that best meets their needs.

What should we know as we develop virtual school libraries?

- "Three-quarters of online teens use instant messaging" (*Teens Technology* 3).
- "Some 57% of online teens create content for the Internet" (*Teen Content* i).
- "Nineteen percent of online teens keep a blog and 38% read them" (*Teen Content* i).
- E-mail, chat, instant messaging, and discussion forums each provide learning experiences and require thinking on the part of students (Tapscott 134).
- Teens use e-mail to communicate with adults and to work with lengthy or complicated information. For the shorter "stuff," they use instant messaging (*Teens Forge* 2).
- "Librarians also need to be more cognizant of Net Gen students' reliance on visual cues using the Internet and build Web pages that are more visually oriented" (Lippincott 13.3). "A study of high school students' Web searching revealed that students relied heavily on information displayed in graphic form on Web pages and

often relied on graphics and visual cues to interpret the relevance of such pages" (Lippincott 13.5).
- "Students also like self-service, interactive Web sites" (Lippincott 13.9). Library media specialists " . . . add value to key pages of their Web sites by including interactive tutorials on how to find information or how to judge quality information resources" (Lippincott 13.9).
- Joyce Valenza notes that students "value such things as access to databases, teacher/librarian recommended links, documentation advice, and readers' advisory" (*Teens and Virtual*).
- "Some 54% of home users have broadband connections" (Rainie 2-3).

Implications

To engage student learners, virtual Web sites we develop should offer interactivity, e-mail/chat/instant messaging ask-a-librarian features, and perhaps even opportunities for blogging. Video and audio streaming are possible due to the number of students with broadband access to the Internet. Our Web pages should provide instruction and guidance as well as information.

Conclusion

As the NCES report, *Fifty Years of Supporting Children's Learning: A History of Public School Libraries and Federal Legislation from 1953 to 2000*, states, "School libraries have evolved from having a primary focus on books to providing a rich array of resources found in the information centers of today" (v). Our collections have changed significantly through the years. However, we have reached a time in which " . . . libraries [need] to rethink their virtual services to provide a better complement to their physically based services" (Lippincott 13.10). We must maximize the information resources that we have and facilitate student usage of these resources.

The perfect opportunity presents itself: "Eighty-six percent of teens, and 88% of online teens, believe that the Internet helps teenagers to do better in school. Eighty percent of parents and 83% of parents of online teens agreed with that proposition" (*Teens Technology* 3). Our students use the Internet, and they believe (and their parents believe) that the Internet improves their academic performance in school. Our libraries must go virtual. "Teachers and students born in the digital age expect digital solutions" (Reid 28).

Lippincott urges library media specialists to "try to think of your library as an environment rather than a facility—a place of interaction, learning, and experiencing rather than a place for storage and equipment" (13.11). "Libraries have been adjusting their collections, services, and environments to the digital world for at least 20 years" (13.1). We must continue to do so to provide virtual library service for our students.

As we began this chapter, we looked at the *Beloit College Mindset List for the Class of 2009*. In this list, Neif notes "libraries have always been the best centers for computer technology and access to good software" (5). We in school libraries must live up to these expectations. We must provide resources in accessible format and services that meet the needs of our very different patrons.

CHAPTER TWO

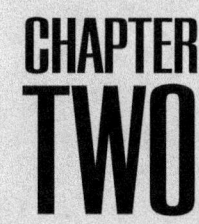

Information Access and Delivery

The Information Content of the Virtual Library

> **From**
> ***Information Power: Building Partnerships for Learning, Chapter 5: Information Access and Delivery . . .***
>
> "Principle 1: The library media program provides intellectual access to information and ideas for learning.
>
> Principle 2: The library media program provides physical access to information and resources for learning.
>
> Principle 3: The library media program provides a climate that is conducive to learning.
>
> Principle 4: The library media program requires flexible and equitable access to information, ideas, and resources for learning" (83).

Reprinted with permission from the American Library Association and American Association of School Librarians.

"All members of the learning community need accurate, current information to meet learning needs, and the school library media specialist takes the lead in locating information and offering guidance in its selection and use" (American Association of School Librarians 84). Through a quality school library media center Web page, the library media specialist can provide accurate and current information that meets student learning needs. With a quality school library media center Web page, the library media specialist exhibits leadership, establishes a virtual presence for the library, presents information, and offers guidance in its use. What should a quality library media center Web page include? Certain key elements should be present: the online catalog, subscription databases (including periodicals, encyclopedias, and specialized subject databases), reference materials, a professional collection for teachers, a section for parents, ebooks, and selected Web sites. We will examine each of these and then conclude with a look at some relatively new and exciting tools that greatly enhance access to information resources.

Online Catalog

Once upon a time, not too many years ago, library catalogs existed in card format and were housed in wooden cabinets with drawers. Access was limited to those patrons physically in the library, and only one student could use a catalog drawer at a time. By the mid-1980s, library circulation systems in the schools expanded to include catalog modules, and online public access catalogs, or OPACs, were born. At first, of course, online catalog access was limited to computers located within the library itself. As local area networks were installed in schools, with a network version of the automation package, catalog access expanded to classrooms and computer labs. Now, automation systems offer Web-accessible OPACs, many of which have multilingual capabilities. On your school library media Web page, you will want to link to your OPAC so that patrons have catalog search capabilities anywhere they have Internet access. Automation systems found in school libraries today typically offer Web components.

- Alexandria <www.goalexandria.com> offers Web-based searching interfaces;
- Athena <www.sagebrushcorp.com/tech/athena.cfm> offers *Athena Web server*;

- Follett <www.fsc.follett.com/products/webcollection_plus/index.cfm> offers *WebCollectionPlus*;
- *SIRSI I-bistro* <www.sirsi.com/Solutions/Prodserv/Products/ibistro.html> provides an enhanced Web-based catalog;
- Spectrum's *Web Catalog* <www.sagebrushcorp.com/tech/spectrum_webcatalog.cfm> provides anytime, anywhere access to the library catalog;
- Surpass *Web-Safari* <www.surpasssoftware.com/websafari-centriva.htm> offers a Web-based catalog; and
- TLC's *CarlWeb* <www.tlcdelivers.com/tlc/carlweb.asp> provides a user-friendly Web gateway to the library's catalog.

Figure 2.1 shows the opening page of the catalog for Chesterfield County Public Schools (VA). Note the options to search by school level or by all schools as well as the multilingual features of the catalog.

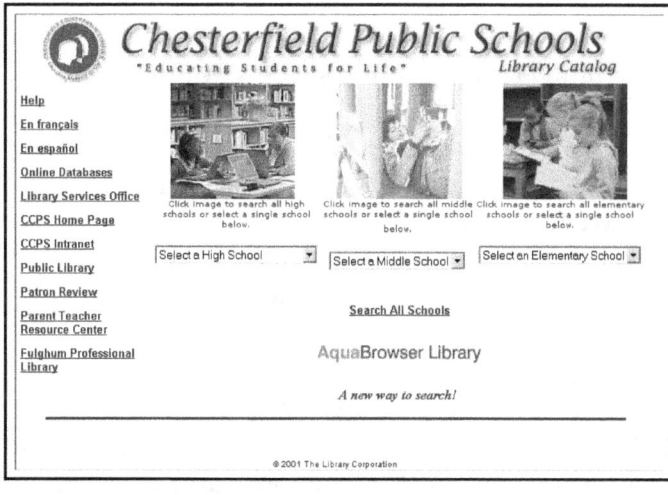

Figure 2.1: Chesterfield County Public Schools TLC OPAC. Reprinted with permission from The Library Corporation.

Whatever automation package you happen to have in place in your library, making the catalog available on the school library Web page will greatly enhance the level of service you provide. With this catalog, you can offer numerous access possibilities:

1. Pre-search: Students can select potential resources by searching the catalog from any location. From home or from the classroom, prior to actually visiting the library,

students can search their topic, select materials they wish to check out, and come with a printout of requested materials in hand.
2. Citation of sources: Likewise, since MARC records contain required bibliographic information, a student completing a works cited page for a project or paper can use the Web-based online catalog to verify (or to fill in gaps) his citations.
3. Access to ebooks: If you subscribe to ebooks, you can make them available via the OPAC. A catalog search for that particular book will then produce the link, allowing the student to directly access the electronic text of the book.
4. Web sites: If you catalog Web sites, you can make them available via the OPAC. For example, for our student, Sarah, researching the planet Saturn, if you have cataloged the Web site for *The Nine Planets: A Multimedia Tour of the Solar System* in your OPAC and put the URL in the 856 MARC field, when Sarah does a subject or keyword search in the catalog for Planets, she will be led to this site.
5. Reading programs: If your school uses a reading program such as *Accelerated Reader* or *Reading Counts* and you load information for reading level, interest level, and points value into the 526 field in the MARC record, students (or parents) can search by reading level, interest level, or points from any location with Internet access.

Subscription Databases

The school library media center Web page should definitely contain links to available subscription databases. Your first step will be to investigate what databases are available to you at the state and then at the district level. Many states provide subscription databases for school libraries. Examples are North Carolina's NCWiseOwl <www.ncwiseowl.org> which features Gale *Infotrac* databases, *Grolier Online*, as well as Gale reference ebooks; Kentucky's Virtual Library <www.kyvl.org> which offers EBSCO databases, *Grolier Online*, and *Wilson Biographies*; Georgia's Galileo <www.Galileo.usg.edu> which offers over 100 databases including EBSCO; and Indiana's INSPIRE <www.inspire.net> which features numerous EBSCO databases. By all means, you should provide access to your state's virtual library databases via your school library Web page so that students and teachers can take easy advantage of these resources.

Additionally, school districts may purchase databases for district-wide use, and you may decide to subscribe to a particular database that you need for your school curriculum and pay for it out of your library budget. In Virginia, for example, the following databases are available to K-12 public schools through FindItVa:

- *Biography Resource Center*
- *Business & Company Resource Center*
- *Computer Database*
- *Contemporary Literary Criticism Select*
- *Expanded Academic ASAP*
- *Gale Virtual Reference Library*
- *General Reference Center–Gold*
- *Health & Wellness Resource Center*
- *Health & Wellness Resource Center Alternative Health Module*
- *InfoTrac Junior Edition*
- *InfoTrac OneFile*
- *InfoTrac OneFile PLUS and Expanded Academic ASAP PLUS*
- *InfoTrac Religion & Philosophy*
- *InfoTrac Student Edition*
- *InfoTrac Kids Bits*
- *LegalTrac*
- *Military & Intelligence Database*
- *K12 Professional Collection*
- *What Do I Read Next?*
- *SIRS Products*
- *SIRS Researcher*
- *SIRS Government Reporter*
- *SIRS Renaissance*
- *SIRS Interactive Citizenship*
- *SIRS Discoverer*
- *eLibrary*

To supplement the state-provided databases, Gloucester County Public Schools (VA) subscribes to *World Book Online* for all schools in the district; Gloucester High School additionally subscribes to *LitFinder: World's Best Poetry*; Facts on File *Science on File* and *Issues & Controversies*; *Taylor's Encyclopedia of Government Officials*; and *ProQuest Learning: Literature* and *History Study Center*. On the other hand, Albemarle County Public Schools (VA) subscribes to *Britannica Online* and *Enciclopedia Universal en Español*; *Grolier Online*; *World Book Online* (for elementary and middle); *Gale Resource Center Gold, Opposing Viewpoints*, and *Science Resource Center* (for high schools); *Gale Resource Center Junior* (for middle schools); EBSCO *Primary Search* (for elementary) and *MiddleSearch* (for middle). Albemarle High School chooses to add *Congressional Quarterly* and *LitFinder* while Western Albemarle High School adds the Gale *World History Resource Center* and *LitFinder*.

Whatever subscription databases are available for your students from whatever funding source, they should be accessible via the school library media center Web page. What types of databases will you include in your virtual library? Consider general periodical, encyclopedia, and subject area specialized databases.

General Periodical Databases

Whether you are at the elementary, middle, or high school level, you will definitely want to provide access to at least one general periodical database.

- EBSCO offers numerous periodical databases for the K-12 environment. For general periodical access, they offer *MAS Ultra—School Edition, Middle Search Plus*, and *Primary Search*. *KidsSearch* and *Searchasaurus* provide child-friendly interfaces to the databases for younger students.
- H.W. Wilson offers *Readers' Guide, Readers' Guide Retrospective: 1890 to 1982*; and Wilson *OmniFile*.
- ProQuest offers *eLibrary* and *ProQuest Platinum*.
- SIRS offers the *SIRS Discoverer* and *SIRS Researcher*.
- Thomson Gale offers *Expanded Academic ASAP, Infotrac OneFile*, and *Kids Infobits*.

General Encyclopedia Databases

Again, whatever grade levels are present in your school, you will want to subscribe to at least one online encyclopedia appropriate for your patrons.

- Encyclopaedia Britannica offers *Britannica Online* and *Britannica Online School Edition* (which includes, among other features, *Britannica*, *Britannica Student*, and *Britannica Elementary*).
- Grolier offers *Encyclopedia Americana*, *Grolier Multimedia Encyclopedia*, *The New Book of Knowledge*, and *La Nueva Enciclopedia Cumbre*.
- World Book offers *World Book Online Reference Center* and *Enciclopedia Estudiantil Hallazgos*.

Subject Area Specialized Databases

As appropriate for your school's grade levels and curriculum support needs, you will want to provide access to specialized subject area databases.

- EBSCO offers a *General Science Collection*, *History Reference Center*, *Vocational & Career Collection*, and a *World History Collection*.
- Encyclopaedia Britannica offers *Annals of American History*.
- Facts on File offers *American History Online*, *World History Online*, *American Women's History*, *African-American History and Culture*, *American Indian History and Culture*, *Ancient History and Culture*, *Health Reference Center*, *Science Online*, and *Literary Reference Online*.
- Greenwood Electronic Media offers *Greenwood Daily Life Online*.
- Grolier offers *The New Book of Popular Science*, *Lands and Peoples*, and *America the Beautiful*.
- H.W. Wilson offers numerous specialized subject area databases and extensive biographical databases including *Biography Reference Bank*.

- ProQuest offers *Culturegrams, eLibrary Science*, ProQuest *AP Science*, ProQuest *Career and Technical Education*, and ProQuest *Historical Newspapers*.
- SIRS offers *SIRS Decades, SIRS Government Reporter*, and *SIRS Renaissance*.
- Thomson Gale offers *Biography Resource Center, Business and Company Resource Center, Discovering Collection, Health and Wellness Resource Center, History Resource Center World, History Resource Center U.S., Literature Resource Center, LitFinder, Opposing Viewpoints Resource Center*, and *Science Resource Center*.

Reference Access

A natural area of opportunity for virtual service on the school library media center Web page is reference. Reference materials in electronic format are available 24/7, outside the library, in some cases for multiple users at a time. (Compare this to print reference materials.)

- *Gale Virtual Reference Library* <www.gale.com/GVRL> provides a choice of over 300 titles—encyclopedias, almanacs, and other reference books—from Thomson Gale, SAGE Publications, John Wiley & Sons, Macmillan Reference USA, and other publishers. MARC records can be loaded into the OPAC; patrons can use Boolean searching in a single ebook or across all the Gale ebook collections; and multiple users can access the reference ebook at one time.
- *Gale Junior Reference Collection* <www.gale.com/pdf/facts/jrcK12.pdf>, designed specifically for middle school students, includes more than 7,000 reference documents from *UXL Biographies, UXL Science, UXL Junior DIScovering Authors, UXL Junior Worldmark Encyclopedia* series, and *UXL Multicultural* in addition to images, audio and video clips, a history timeline, and several dictionaries.
- Follett: A search on Follett's *Titlewave* using the selection criteria of "ebook" and "reference" for interest level rated "kindergarten through young adult" produces 34 works, ranging from *American Ethnic Writers* (Salem Press, 2000)

to *Encyclopedia of the Supreme Court* (Facts on File, 2005) to the *Young Person's Occupational Outlook Handbook* (JIST Works, 2003). Comparable in price to their print counterparts, students would access them via the OPAC.
- You may also want to provide links to good reference portals such as the *Internet Public Library* <www.ipl.org> and the *Librarians' Index to the Internet* <www.lii.org>.

Professional Collection

Another tremendous area of opportunity for virtual service is the professional collection. If your teachers never have time and never take advantage of the wonderful (and expensive) resources that you provide in the professional collection, virtual may be the answer. Set up a professional library section on the school library media center Web page with access 24/7 at the point of need from home, school, or any Internet location.

What will you provide in the professional collection section? Teachers are most appreciative if you provide links to **professional organizations** such as the National Council for Social Studies <www.ncss.org>, National Council for Teachers of English <www.ncte.org>, National Council for Teachers of Mathematics <www.nctm.org>, the International Reading Association <www.ira.org>, National Science Teachers' Association <www.nsta.org>, American Council on the Teaching of Foreign Languages <www.actfl.org>, the Council for Exceptional Children <www.cec.sped.org>, and the Alliance for Physical Education, Health, Recreation, and Dance <www.aahperd.org>.

Another area to which teachers appreciate ready access is **links to state department of education** information, particularly information dealing with standards, testing, and assessment. For example, links to Virginia's Standards of Learning and accompanying curriculum framework documents <www.doe.virginia.gov/VDOE/Superintendent/Sols/home.shtml> as well as links to the SOL Test Blueprints <www.doe.virginia.gov/VDOE/Assessment/soltests/home.html> and Released Items from previous administrations of the tests <www.doe.virginia.gov/VDOE/Assessment/releasedtests.html> are very useful to busy classroom teachers. The school library Web page can provide that easy access to needed information.

You will want to provide links to **Web sites** that will assist teachers in their teaching. Some excellent examples follow:

- *The Educator's Reference Desk* (formerly AskERIC) <www.eduref.org> provides 2,000+ links to lesson plans, 3,000+ links to online education information, and 200+ question archive responses.
- *EduScapes: A Site for Life-Long Learners of All Ages* <www.eduscapes.com> Developed by Annette Lamb and Larry Johnson, this site includes 4 2 eXplore, Teacher Tap, Literature Learning Ladders, Information Inquiry for Teachers, Naturescapes, and more.
- *GEM: Gateway to Educational Materials* <www.thegateway.org> is "a Consortium effort to provide quick and easy access to thousands of educational resources found on various federal, state, university, non-profit, and commercial Internet sites."
- *Kathy Schrock's Guide for Educators* <school.discovery.com/schrockguide> "is a categorized list of sites useful for enhancing curriculum and professional growth." Schrock organizes information under Subject Access, Search Tools, Teachers Helpers, and Schrockguide Stuff.
- *Library of Congress Learning Page (Especially for Teachers)* <www.loc.gov/learn> includes "lessons, features, activities, and tips and tricks" to help teachers to effectively use the more than 7 million items in the American Memory collections.
- *The National Digital Science Library* <ndsl.org> Funded by the National Science Foundation, this site provides a digital library of resources, collections, and services, organized to support science education at all levels.

Professional ebooks

- Follett: A search on Follett's *Titlewave* using the criteria of "ebook" and "professional" produces 817 titles, ranging from *Action Research for Inclusive Education* (Routledge Falmer, 2004) to *Key Issues for Secondary Schools*

(RoutledgeFalmer, 2001) to *Youth, Education and Risk* (Taylor and Francis, 2001).
- Greenwood <ebooks.greenwood.com> offers titles such as *Making a Place for Kids with Disabilities* (Praeger, 2000), *Rethinking Issues in Special Education* (Ablex, 2002), and *Using Literature to Help Troubled Teenagers Cope with Societal Issues* (Greenwood, 1999).
- NetLibrary <www.oclc.org/info/k12subjectsets> now offers Subject Sets, bundled sets of ebooks, for *K-6 Teacher's Resources* (such as *Classroom Management that Works*, ASCD, 2003 and *Science through Children's Literature,* Teacher Ideas Press, 2000) and for *7-12 Teacher's Resources* (such as *190 Ready-to-Use Activities that Make Math Fun,* John Wiley & Sons, 2003 and *Uncovering Our History: Teaching with Primary Sources,* ALA Editions, 2004).

Journal Access for Professional Development

EBSCO's *Professional Development* collection contains 729 serials, 549 of which are full text. ProQuest's *Professional Education* collection contains over 300 full text journals, and ProQuest *Education Journals* collection contains over 500 full-text journals. Thomson Gale also offers a *Professional Collection* of journals. Imagine how your teachers will react, having 24/7 online access to all this professional material.

Parents' Space

Providing a Parents' Space on the school library media center Web page does wonders for public relations and parental support and advocacy for the library program. What should you include in this area? Consider the following:

- Links to school policies
- Links to school district policies
- Links to relevant state department of education sites, such as those related to standardized testing
- Links to sites that focus on libraries, reading, and children (such as the *Association for Library Service to Children Resources* <www.ala.org/alsc/parents.links.html>, *Jim Trelease*

on Reading <www.trelease-on-reading.com/>, and Cynthia Leitich Smith's *Children's and Young Adult Literature Resources* <www.cynthialeitichsmith.com/lit_resources/cyalr_index.html>)
- Links to sites that focus on libraries, the Internet, and children (such as the *American Library Association's Online Resources for Parents and Children* <www.ala.org/ala/oif/iftoolkits/litoolkit/onlineresources.htm> and *Indiana University's Clearinghouse on Reading, English, and Communication's Parent Link List* <reading.indiana.edu/www/indexfr.html>)

Ebooks (Fee and Free)
Fee
Several companies now provide ebooks for the K-12 environment, among them Follett, Greenwood, and NetLibrary.

- Follett <www.flr.follett.com> offers 2,500 ebooks, both fiction and nonfiction titles, appropriate for grades K-12, from Brenda Haugen's *The 100th Day of School* (Picture Window Books, 2004; grades K-3) to Patrice Cassedy's *Law Enforcement* (Lucent Books, 2002; grades 5-8) to Libal Autumn's *Women in the Mediterranean World* (Mason Crest Publishers, 2005, YA).
- Greenwood <ebooks.greenwood.com> currently has approximately 300 ebooks available that are appropriate for the 9-12 environment, in addition to some professional titles that would be useful.
- NetLibrary <www.oclc.org/info/k12subjectsets> offers bundled sets of ebooks, K-6 School Resources, K-6 Activities and Experiments, 7-12 Young Adult (YA) School Resources, and a K-12 Spanish Collection. Sample titles from these sets include the following:
  - K-6 *The Kid's Invention Book* (Lerner, 1997) and *Malcolm X: His Life and Legacy* (Millbrook, 1995)
  - 7-12 *Exploring Careers: A Young Person's Guide to 1000 Jobs* (Jist Publications, 2003)
  - K-12 Spanish *Historia de la Yegua Blanca* (CIDCLI, 1994) and *Los Cereales* (Lerner, 2003)

Free
Numerous free ebooks sites are available.

- *Project Gutenberg* <www.gutenberg.org> is the oldest producer of ebooks on the Internet, providing access to 17,000 free ebooks. Sample titles include H.G. Wells' *The War of the Worlds* and Jane Austen's *Pride and Prejudice*.
- *Bartleby.com* <www.bartleby.com> features great books of reference, verse, fiction, and nonfiction. Titles include the 20th edition of *Gray's Anatomy*, Robert Frost's *Miscellaneous Poems to 1920*, and Guy de Maupassant's *The Necklace*.
- *The International Children's Digital Library* <www.childrenslibrary.org> provides an online library for the world's children—874 books written in 33 languages. Sample titles include *The Red Ball* by Farideh Kahlatbari, *People of Salmon and Cedar* by Ron Hirschi, and *Abunuwasi* by GADO.

Searching for a book in electronic format? Try the *Digital Book Index* <www.digitalbookindex.org>, which provides links to over 114,000 ebooks, 75,000 of which are free.

Web Site Subscriptions

If you subscribe to a collection of educational Web sites, you will certainly want to provide access via your virtual library. Some of the current products available follow:

- *Marco Polo* <www.marcopolosearch.org> provides free access to high-quality standards-based Internet content for various disciplines in grades K-12.
- *Web Feet* <www.gale.com/pdf/facts/WebFeetK12.pdf> offers educator-selected, curriculum-related Web sites, available either through MARC records loaded into the OPAC or a user-friendly Web interface. Collections are available in the following clusters: K-8, Core, K-12, or Health.
- *Nettrekker* <www.nettrekker.com> features links to over 180,000 educator-selected online resources aligned with a

state's standards. It is now even available in differentiated instruction format organized by readability level.
- *Web MARC* <www.sagebrushcorp.com/tech/webmarc.cfm> offers more than 6,000 curriculum-related, librarian-selected Web sites that can be seamlessly integrated into and searched through the library catalog.
- *SKS WebSelect* <www.proquestk12.com/pic/pdfs/webselect datasheet.pdf> contains 13,000-plus links appropriate for grades 9-14; links are curriculum-related and topic-organized and entries include an editor-prepared summary to assist students in selecting the most appropriate resource for their information need.
- *Discoverer WebFind* <www.proquestk12.com/pic/pdfs/web selectdatasheet.pdf> contains 5,000-plus links appropriate for grades 1-9, topic-organized with editor-written summaries to facilitate usage.

If your library subscribes to one of the Web site subscription products, it should be available through the library media center Web page either through the OPAC or as a clickable link.

Locally Selected Web Sites

In addition to (or perhaps instead of) purchasing a collection of pre-selected Web sites, you may choose to provide a section on your Web page of quality Web sites appropriate and useful for your patrons. What to include here? Certainly, you will want to include links to dictionary and ready reference sites.

Sample Dictionary Sites
- *Dictionary.com* <dictionary.reference.com> includes *AHD*, 4th ed, Webster's Revised Unabridged Dictionary, and others; sister site is *Thesaurus.com*.
- *OneLook Dictionaries* <www.onelook.com> allows you to search for multiple definitions of a word from a variety of online dictionaries.
- *YourDictionary.com* <www.yourdictionary.com> includes dictionary and thesaurus, plus multilingual and "nyms and such."

Sample Ready Reference Sites
- *Information Please Almanac* <www.infoplease.com> offers millions of useful and interesting facts on a wide range of topics.
- *Farmer's Almanac* <www.farmersalmanac.com> includes weather forecasts, gardening and fishing calendars, household tips, best days, and recipes.
- *World Almanac for Kids* <www.worldalmanacforkids.com/> offers games, quizzes, contests, and reference facts on topics like space, presidents, the environment, and animals.
- *CIA World Fact Book* <www.cia.gov/cia/publications/factbook/> is a government sponsored site, giving country profiles, facts, and reference maps.
- *Occupational Outlook Handbook* <stats.bls.gov/oco/home.htm> is a government sponsored site, giving basic information about various careers and occupations.
- *Bartlett's Familiar Quotations* <www.bartleby.com/100/> 10th ed., 1919, of Bartlett's famous work, includes over 11,000 searchable quotations.

In your section of locally selected Web sites, you may also want to include biographical, geographical, and government links.

Sample Biographical Links
- *Biography.com* <www.biography.com/> affiliated with Arts and Entertainment, over 25,000 of the greatest lives, past and present
- *Michigan Electronic Library Reference Desk: Biography* <web.mel.org/viewtopic.jsp?id=336&pathid=1133> reference desk from MEL, links to numerous biography items
- *POTUS: Presidents of the United States* <ipl.si.umich.edu/div/potus/> biographies of the Presidents

Sample Geographical Links
- *Atlases: National Atlas of the United States of America* <www.nationalatlas.gov/> numerous topographical maps of the country and individual states
- *Country Information: U.S. State Department—Country Profiles* <www.state.gov/r/pa/ei/bgn/> statistics and history of government entities and international organizations
- *Maps: Mapquest* <www.mapquest.com> maps and directions to almost anywhere
- *Maps: Rand McNally Travel Directions* <www.randmcnally.com/> maps, directions, and road trip planning
- *Maps: United Nations Cartographic Section* <www.un.org/Depts/Cartographic/english/htmain.htm> maps and geographic information resources: general maps and peacekeeping maps
- *Gazetteer: United States Gazetteer* <www.census.gov/cgi-bin/gazetteer> United States Census Bureau, search for United States places
- *Travel: Fodor's* <www.fodors.com/> destinations, hotels, restaurants, tipping, and more

Sample Government Sites, Federal
- *Firstgov.gov* <firstgov.gov/> The United States Government's Official Web Portal
- *American Memory Project* <memory.loc.gov/ammem/> historical collections for the national digital library at the Library of Congress
- *Ben's Guide to Government for Kids* <bensguide.gpo.gov/> government for K-2, 3-5, 6-8, 9-12
- *FedStats.gov* <www.fedstats.gov/> the gateway to statistics from over 100 U.S. federal agencies
- *Medline Plus Health Information* <medlineplus.gov/> a service of the United States National Library of Medicine and the National Institutes of Health
- *NASA* <www.nasa.gov/home/index.html> National Aeronautics and Science Administration
- *National Center for Education Statistics* <nces.ed.gov/> the primary federal entity for collecting and analyzing data

that are related to education in the United States and other nations
- *Statistical Abstract of the United States* <www.census.gov/statab/www/> a collection of statistics on social and economic conditions in the United States, with selected international data as well

You will, of course, also want to provide links to state and local government sites. For these sites, consider including the following: links to the official state and local government sites, links to state and local public libraries, and links to state and local district education sites.

What else to consider? According to Joyce Valenza's research, "students wanted the following and much more: world news/current events, more booklists, more details for English and social studies, easy links to online reference, college stuff, career stuff, government and economics, more support for research papers" (*Teens and Virtual*).

Federated or Meta Searching

Many of our electronic resources now provide multiple access options. For example, ebooks from both Greenwood and Thomson Gale may be loaded and accessible via a list of ebooks on the Web page or via MARC records in the OPAC. Soon, we will not only provide links to our catalogs on our library Web pages, but also the capability of one-stop information shopping across electronic resources, one-stop information shopping that our patrons have come to expect from using search tools on the Web. The following products all offer federated searching capabilities. Federated searching, as defined by the *Online Dictionary of Library and Information Science*, is "a search for information using software designed to query multiple networked information resources via a single interface."

- *Follett One-Search* <www.fsc.follett.com/files/pdf/fiac_detail_10545a.pdf> facilitates a single search across both free services and databases from ABC-CLIO, EBSCO, Facts on File, ProQuest, Thomson Gale, World Book, and others.

- *Thomson Gale Power Search* <www.gale.com/Technical/> offers patrons the capability of searching across all Gale products to which the library subscribes—all ebooks purchased from the *Gale Virtual Library* plus content in the *Infotrac* periodical databases.
- *TLC WebFeat* <www.tlcdelivers.com/tlc/partnerships.asp?tpId=27&#partners> simultaneously searches the online catalog, free Internet services, and subscription-based databases.
- *SIRSI SingleSearch* <www.sirsi.com/Solutions/Prodserv/Products/ibistro.html> simultaneously searches local collections, other libraries' catalogs, Web search engines, journals, and databases.

Access from within *Blackboard*

If your school subscribes to a course management software program such as *Blackboard*, you might consider developing a virtual library presence there. One advantage of providing access via a *Blackboard* site is that *Blackboard* is password protected. Because only authorized users can log in to *Blackboard*, subscription databases, user IDs, and passwords can be given within *Blackboard*. Another advantage of using *Blackboard* is "local control," which we will address more fully in our chapter on program administration.

Virginia Palmen, Library Media Specialist at Lee-Davis High School in Hanover County, Virginia, shares the following:

> My site is set up as a class, and my class name is Lee-Davis Library. All students and teachers are enrolled as students. The Databases/Web sites section includes links, descriptions, and passwords to our subscription databases. I use the *Blackboard* when instructing students how to access databases, pathfinders, and other Web sites. I also use *Blackboard* to attach conference handouts for presentations I do, documents, notes, etc. that I need to get to faculty because I'm our Technology Coach. We try to make our Web site simple and include only things that don't change because it's very hard to make changes. They have to be

approved, and the Web administrator has to actually make the change. Our Web site links to *Blackboard*, and our *Blackboard* links to the Web site. We actually use the *Blackboard* for instruction.

Of course, there are advantages to using such a course management system to deliver library information sources and services. User IDs and passwords can be made easily available; another advantage is the library's presence in *Blackboard*. Typically, students use *Blackboard* for content area coursework. Having a *Blackboard* library course raises the library's instructional status to that of a classroom. It is important, however, to maintain a basic Web presence for the library, one that is openly accessible to all. Patrons and outsiders will judge the library by your Web site, so one should exist on the free Internet. The two, as Palmen notes, can complement each other.

Conclusion

As we develop or enhance the school library media center Web page to provide a virtual presence for our library, we pay careful attention to providing intellectual and physical access to appropriate information and to library resources. We include links to our online catalog, subscription databases (including periodicals, encyclopedias, and specialized subject databases), reference materials, a professional collection for teachers, a space for parents, ebooks, and selected Web sites. We may offer one-stop information shopping for our patrons via federated searching, and we may choose to provide more complete access to resources via a course management system such as *Blackboard*. Our library must have a virtual presence on the Web to provide readily accessible information for our students and teachers.

Exemplary Web Pages for Information Access and Delivery
(Selected for the quality of intellectual and physical access to information which they provide)

Greece Athena Media Center, Rochester, NY
<www.greece.k12.ny.us/ath/library/>

Winner of IASL/Concord School Library Web Page of the Month—Includes Online Databases, Teacher Projects, Research Guide, Teacher Resources, Virtual Reading Room, News Links, Webmaster Workshop, Middle School Homepage, Reference Desk, OPAC, Bibliography Guide, Summer Reading List, Link to Local Public Library, Internet Safety, WebQuests, and High School Homepage.

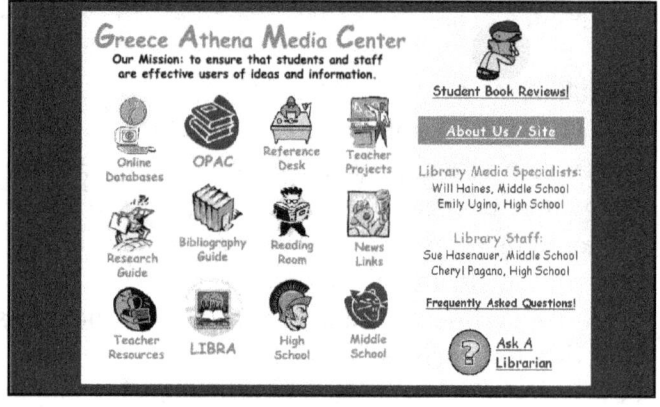

Figure.2.2: Greece Athena Media Center Web page, Rochester, NY. Reprinted with permission from Will Haines, Greece Athena Middle School, School Librarian.

Walter Reed Middle School Library, Los Angeles, CA
<www.lausd.k12.ca.us/Reed_MS/Library/>
 Includes Online Catalog, Online Resources, Curricular Links, About the Library, Using the Library, Book Talk, Research Process, Reed Homepage, and LAUSD Digital Library.

Figure 2.3: Walter Reed Middle School Library Web page. Reprinted with permission from Mark L. Bobrosky, Walter Reed Middle School, Library Media Teacher.

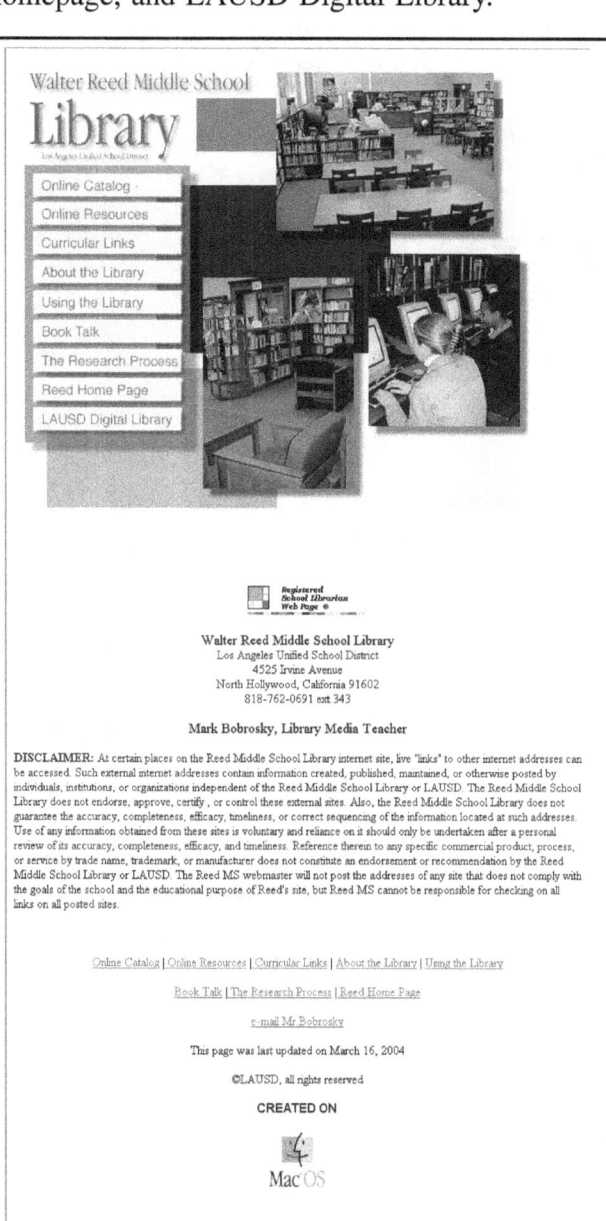

Chapter 2: Information Access and Delivery

The Paideia School Library, Atlanta, GA
<www.paideiaschool.org/library/default.htm>
> Includes About the Library, Databases, Reading, Search Engines, Search the Library Catalog, Recommended Web Sites (grouped by subject in their Dewey Decimal categories), Research Guides, Family Resources, and Teacher Resources.

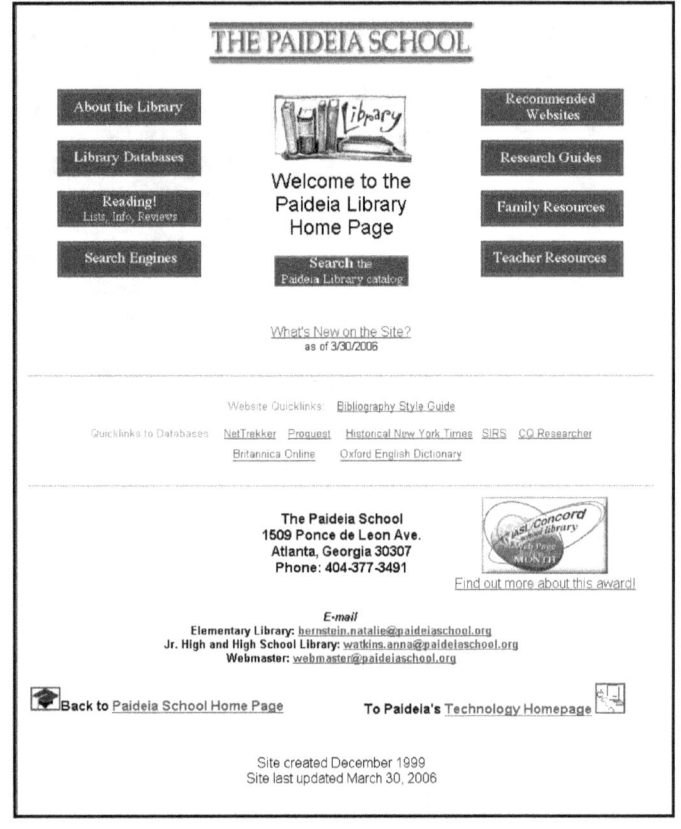

Figure 2.4: Paideia School Library Web page. Reprinted with permission from Natalie Bernstein, Paideia School Library, Elementary Librarian.

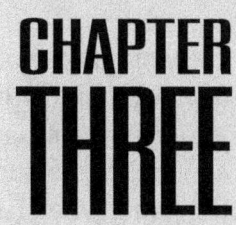

CHAPTER THREE

Learning and Teaching
What It Is All About

> **From**
>
> ***Information Power: Building Partnerships for Learning, Chapter 4: Learning and Teaching . . .***
>
> "Principle 5: Access to the full range of information resources and services through the library media program is fundamental to learning.
>
> Principle 8: The library media program fosters individual and collaborative inquiry.
>
> Principle 9: The library media program integrates the uses of technology for teaching and learning.
>
> Principle 10: The library media program is an essential link to the larger learning community" (58).

Reprinted with permission from the American Library Association and American Association of School Librarians.

"Schools have evolved to focus on learning, and effective school library media programs have also changed their focus from collections to learning that engages students in pursuing knowledge within and beyond a formal curriculum" (American Association of School Librarians 59). Providing virtual library services hinges upon providing access and delivery to quality information resources; providing access and delivery, however, is necessary but not sufficient. In addition to making information readily available, it is the responsibility of the school library media specialist to teach and assist students in learning how to use these information resources. In a face-to-face environment, we teach information literacy skills in connection with content area curriculum at the point of need. In a virtual environment, we must strive to provide that same quality of information literacy skills instruction.

> **Information literacy**
> ...the ability to recognize a need for information, to access information efficiently and effectively, to evaluate information critically and competently, and to use information accurately and creatively (*Information Power: Building Partnerships for Learning*).

Students using our library media center Web site as an access point for information have recognized the need for information. As a library media specialist working in a virtual environment, our next challenge is to help them access, evaluate, and use that information. How do we go about that? Certainly, we must pay attention to what research has shown about youth and Web use concerning interactivity. Wherever possible, we should include interactive elements on this portion of the school library media center Web site. We can make use of tutorials to teach information literacy skills.

What types of teaching and learning activities should be included? This chapter will focus on curriculum support (pathfinders and WebQuests), information literacy instruction (basic instruction in information literacy, effective use of search tools, evaluating Web sites, the research process, intellectual property, and citations of sources), reading (including library blogs), and virtual reference services (ask-a-librarian via e-mail, chat, or instant messaging).

Curriculum Support

A key area which our school library Web page should address is that of curriculum support. One of the primary goals of a school library is to support the instructional program of the school; any online assistance that we can provide related to the content area curriculums will be greatly appreciated by students and teachers alike. In fact, research shows that "higher performing school library media specialists and programs may be a function of a more enriching learning environment that includes a supportive administration, collaborative teachers, and an up-to-date resource and technology base" (*School Libraries Work* 9). A significant way in which we can support classroom instruction and enhance the learning environment is through pathfinders, and these pathfinders should be developed in collaboration with classroom teachers.

> **Pathfinders**
>
> **pathfinder** (as defined in the *Online Dictionary for Library and Information Science*, <lu.com/odlis/odlis_p.cfm>): A subject bibliography designed to lead the user through the process of researching a specific topic, or any topic in a given field or discipline, usually in a systematic, step-by-step way, making use of the best finding tools the library has to offer. Pathfinders may be printed or available online. See also: topical guide.

Reprinted with permission from Joan M. Reitz.

Pathfinders

Some excellent examples of pathfinders can be found at the following sites:

- *John Newbery Elementary School Library Media Center Pathfinders for Grades K-5,* Wenatchee, WA <nb.wsd.wednet.edu/lmc/pathfinders/pathfinder.htm>. Ranging from "Trees" and "Weather" for kindergarten to the "Lewis and Clark Expedition" and "Electricity" for grade 4 to "Colonial America" for grade 5, these attractive pathfinders guide and support the research efforts of our younger students.

- *Middle School Pathfinders from Lakewood Public Library for Lakewood Public Schools,* Lakewood, OH <www.lkwdpl.org/schools/midschl.htm>. With topics ranging from "Arab Cultural Arts Day" to the "El Niño Project "to "Types of Government/Branches of Government," these pathfinders offer links to selected Internet resources appropriate for the topic. While these pathfinders are limited to online resources and do not include subscription databases or print materials, they represent a tremendous collaborative effort between the Lakewood, Ohio public library and the school system.
- *Springfield Township High School Library*, Erdenheim, PA <mciu.org/%7Espjvweb/pathmenu.html>. Joyce Valenza provides pathfinders for topics as varied as "Literary Criticism," "Nations and Travel," "College Search," and "Health and Diseases."

WebQuests

You may want to feature curriculum-related WebQuests on your school library media Web page. As defined by Bernie Dodge, Professor of Educational Technology at San Diego State University and Creator of the WebQuest model, a WebQuest is "an inquiry-oriented activity in which some or all of the information that learners interact with comes from resources on the Internet." Certainly WebQuests offer to students the ultimate in interactivity.

Sources of WebQuests follow:

- *WebQuest Portal*, Bernie Dodge, San Diego State University <www.webquest.org>. The official page from the father of WebQuests, this site offers more than 2,500 quality Web sites and is searchable by keyword, content area, and grade level.
- *BestWebQuests.com*, Tom March <bestwebquests.com/>. This site offers the best WebQuests available (just under 200 of the almost 1,200 reviewed), searchable by content area and learner's age.

Information Literacy Skills Instruction
Basic Instruction in Information Literacy:
Via your school library media Web page, you will want to offer students the opportunity to gain basic information literacy skills. Following are general information literacy tutorials available on the Web that you might include:

- *21st Century Literacies* <www.kn.pacbell.com/wired/21stcent/gradelevel.html>. Offers information literacy skills lessons, arranged by grade level, from Brainstorming Research Questions for K-2 to Online Search Techniques for grades 6-12.
- *KidsClick: Search Tools*, Ramapo Catskill Library System <www.rcls.org/wows/>. Designed for our younger students, offers a step-by-step overview for searching on the Web, including advice for using keywords effectively and for using Boolean logic.

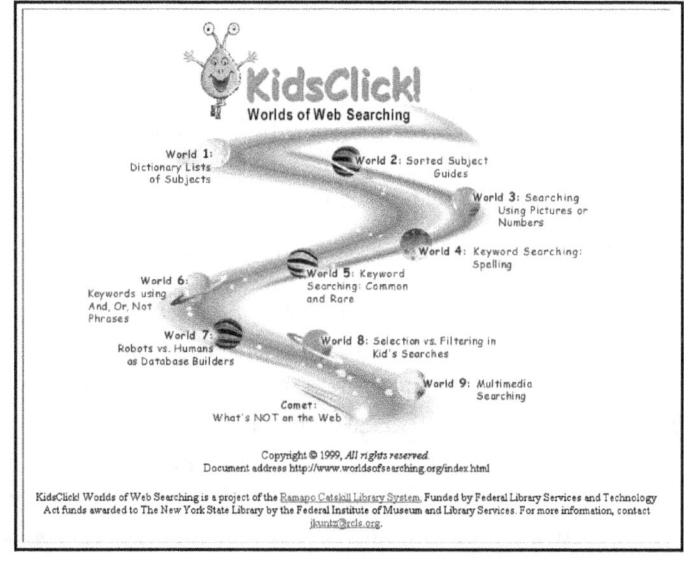

Figure 3.1: KidsClick! Worlds of Web Searching. Reprinted with permission from Jerry Kuntz, Ramapo Catskill Library System.

- *TILT: Texas Information Literacy Tutorial*, University of Texas System Digital Library <tilt.lib.utsystem.edu>. Designed for grades 8 and up, this library tutorial, available in TILT Lite (no plug-ins required) or Full TILT (which

offers full interactivity) prepares students to conduct research online by focusing on fundamental research skills.
- *Finding Information on the Internet: A Tutorial*, University of California, Berkeley <www.lib.berkeley.edu/TeachingLib/Guides/Internet/FindInfo.html>. Also for older students, this tutorial addresses effective searching, evaluating information found, and citing sources.
- *Information Literacy and You,* Penn State University Libraries <www.libraries.psu.edu/instruction/infolit/andyou/infoyou.htm>. Again, for older students, this tutorial guides the student from definition of topic to searching to evaluating to citing.
- *Online Lessons,* Springfield Township High School Library, Erdenheim, PA <mciu.org/~spjvweb/jvles.html>. Joyce Valenza has collected numerous information literacy lessons; select the lessons that are appropriate for students in your school, and link them on your school library Web page.

Effective Use of Search Tools:

To search effectively, students must use appropriate search tools. On your school library media Web page, you will need to provide links not only to search tools, but also to lessons or tutorials that help students to use these search tools effectively. The following sites may be useful:

- *Choosing Search Tools: Debbie Abilock's Choose the Best Search for Your Information Need* <www.noodletools.com/debbie/literacies/information/5locate/adviceengine.html>. Offers a chart to assist the user in choosing a search tool appropriate for a particular information need.
- *Oregon School Library Information System Beyond Surfing* <www.oslis.k12.or.us/secondary/index.php?page=beyondSurfing>. Discusses directories, search engines, metasearch engines, and portals, and then offers a self-check.

To search effectively on the Web, students must understand Boolean logic.

- *Online Search Techniques,* M.W. Bell Library, Guilford Technical Community College, Jamestown, NC <webster.gtcc.cc.nc.us/library/searchtechniques.html>. Explains this concept in simple terms with excellent diagrams.
- *Boolean Searching on the Internet,* University of Albany State University of New York <library.albany.edu/internet/boolean.html>. Includes basic information about the Boolean operators, gives clear examples, and discusses Boolean operators in the context of search tools.
- *TALON: Taking Libraries Online Tutorial,* Simpson Library, University of Mary Washington, Fredericksburg, VA <www.library.umw.edu/talon/outline.html>. Takes students through the research process, step-by-step.

Evaluating Web Sites:
Once students find sites on the Web, they certainly need to be able to evaluate what they have found. Following are sites that offer Web evaluation tools:

- *ICYouSee: T is for Thinking: The ICYouSee Guide to Critical Thinking About What You See on the Web*, Ithaca College Library, Ithaca, NY <www.ithaca.edu/library/training/think.html>. Interactive and user-friendly, this site encourages critical evaluation of information found on the Web.
- *QUICK: Quality Information Checklist* <www.quick.org.uk/menu.htm>. Appropriate for older elementary and middle school students; eight interactive questions help students judge the quality of information found.
- *Kathy Schrock's Critical Evaluation of a Web Page Tool for Elementary, Middle, and High Schools* <school.discovery.com/schrockguide/evalelem.html>, <school.discovery.com/schrockguide/evalmidd.html>, <school.discovery.com/schrockguide/evalhigh.html>. Evaluation guides in html, pdf, and Word format for each grade level.

- *Five Criteria for Evaluating Web sites*, Cornell University Library, Ithaca, NY <www.library.cornell.edu/olinuris/ref/webcrit.html>. Developed by Cornell University Libraries, this easy-to-read chart offers questions to ask for the five criteria for evaluation.
- *Loogootee Elementary West Evaluation Rubrics for Web sites*, Loogootee, IN <www.siec.k12.in.us/%7Ewest/online/eval.htm>. Offers Web evaluation tools for elementary, intermediate, and secondary grades.

The Research Process: Research Guides

Research is a complex process for students, and they depend on library media specialists to guide them through that process. When students are working in a virtual environment, we must strive to provide that same guidance that we provide face to face. Sites such as the following, linked on the school library Web page, will facilitate this guidance:

- *OSLIS/Oregon School Library Information System Middle and High School* <www.oslis.k12.or.us/secondary/index.php>. Gives a step-by-step interactive tutorial, including self-checks, from beginning the research process to presenting results.
- *OSLIS/Oregon School Library Information System Elementary* <www.oslis.k12.or.us/elementary/index.php>. Gives a step-by-step interactive tutorial, including self-checks from the beginning—do research, to the end—cite sources.
- *How to Do Research*, Kentucky Virtual Library <www.kyvl.org/html/tutorial/research/>. This tutorial addresses doing research, finding articles, finding books, searching the Web, evaluating information, citing sources.
- *Research Rocket*, Kentucky Virtual Library <www.kyvl.org/html/kids/portal.html>. This tutorial is designed especially for elementary students to learn how to explore "All the Information in the Known Universe."

Figure 3.2: Research Rocket, Kentucky Virtual Library. Reprinted with permission from the Kentucky Virtual Library, Enid Wohlstein, Director.

- *KCTools, A KidsConnect Research Toolbox*, American Association of School Librarians <www.ala.org/ala/aasl/schlibrariesandyou/k12students/aaslkctools.htm>. Guides students through the basic steps in research—I Wonder, I Find, I Evaluate, I Share.
- *Greece Athena Media Research Guide (Big 6™): Getting It Done—Six Steps to Success*, Rochester, NY <www.greece.k12.ny.us/ath/library/bigsix/default.htm>. Six steps, based on the Big Six™, serve as a guide to the research process.
- *Walter Reed Middle School Library Research Process Overview*, Los Angeles, CA <www.lausd.k12.ca.us/Reed_MS/Library/research/research.html>. Walks students, step-by-step, through the research process.

Citations and Ethical Use of Information

Students must understand the concept of intellectual property and copyright. On the school library media center Web page, we must stress the importance of citing sources, and we must provide instruction for students in how to do so.

- *Nauset Public Schools*, Orleans, MA <nausetschools.org/research/works2.htm>. Provides bibliographic citation formats for grades 1-6.
- *OSLIS/Oregon School Library Information System Citation Maker for Elementary* (based on MLA Style) <www.oslis.k12.or.us/elementary/index.php?page=citeSources>. Discusses how to cite sources and includes a link to citation maker.
- *OSLIS/Oregon School Library Information System Secondary Citing Sources* (based on MLA Style) <www.oslis.k12.or.us/secondary/index.php?page=citeSources>. Offers a link to citation maker as well as guidance on such topics as when to cite, plagiarism, and note taking skills.

It is also very helpful to students if they have bibliographic style guides available on the school library media Web page. The following sites provide guidance for students in this area:

- *Style Guide for Research Project Documentation*, Paideia School Library, Atlanta, GA <www.paideiaschool.org/library/research/styleguide.htm>. This page explains the importance of documentation and citation and then gives examples.
- *How to Cite Sources,* John Newbery Elementary School Library Media Center, Wenatchee, WA <nb.wsd.wednet.edu/lmc/lmc_citingsources.htm>. This attractive, user-friendly site gives examples of how to cite sources for grades 2-5.
- *Citation Style for Research Papers*, B. Davis Schwartz Memorial Library, Long Island University, Brookville, NY <www.liunet.edu/cwis/cwp/library/workshop/citation.htm>. For the older students, this site gives examples from APA, MLA, Chicago, Turabian, and others, plus it is color-coded and very user friendly.
- *Style Manuals & Writing Guides*, University Library, California State, Los Angeles <www.calstatela.edu/library/styleman.htm>. This site also gives examples from the

various citation formats, but an added bonus is a printable guide for each in either Word or pdf format.

Reading Promotion

The school library media center Web page offers multiple opportunities to promote books and reading. Many OPACs now offer "Amazon.com-like" features: book covers, table of contents, sneak-peeks at first chapters, portions of book reviews, most checked-out book this week, and "if you liked this, you might like this." On the school library media center Web page, the possibilities for reading support and promotion are almost limitless—from book lists to online book reviews to online book clubs and discussions facilitated by blogs. The following library sites feature strong reading elements:

- *Joyce Kilmer Elementary School Media Center,* Mahwah, NJ <www.mahwah.k12.nj.us/jk/mediacenter/index.htm>. This site offers links to favorite authors, books, and series; favorite authors' Web sites; literature and reference links; Newbery, Caldecott, and other award-winning booklists; Accelerated Reader titles; and summer reading lists.
- *Greece Athena Media Center Virtual Reading Room,* Rochester, NY <www.greece.k12.ny.us/ath/library/reading_room/default.htm>. This middle/high school site offers the summer reading list; book and award lists/recommended reading; noted authors and illustrators; for parents: reading with your children; for teachers: promote reading; write a book review (by completing a template and clicking Submit), and read submitted book reviews; tips for selecting books; and news and newspapers.
- *Reading Rants and Raves, BookBreak! Berkley High School Book Blog* <www.bookbreak.blogspot.com/>. Library media specialist Martha J. Spear hosts BookBreak! A Blog for Readers and encourages comments about students' latest reading.
- *Ann Arbor District Library Teen Blogs*, Ann Arbor, MI <www.aadl.org/services/axis>. The Ann Arbor District Library offers a blog for book discussion.

Virtual Librarian Services

If we are to provide virtual services for our patrons, 24 hours a day, seven days a week, we must consider technology-facilitated one-on-one interaction with students in need of assistance. This interaction can be accomplished via e-mail, chat, or instant messaging, and the following sites offer examples of how it can be done:

- *Rochester City School Libraries Ask-A-Librarian*, Rochester, NY <rochestersls.rcsdk12.org/ask.htm>. Rochester City School Librarians are available via e-mail to answer questions regarding library and Internet resources. The librarians will answer the question the next weekday or within 24 hours.
- *Oregon Libraries Network L-net Chat* <live.247ref.org/wcscgi/CDM.exe?SS_COMMAND=CUST_SUP&Category=OR_K_12&VIRTCATEGORY=OR_ORSCHOOLS>. This service is provided for all residents of Oregon; the patron enters such basic information as name, zip code, and grade and clicks Connect. Using chat and co-browsing software, a librarian on duty provides reference assistance.
- *Maryland AskUsNow* <www.askusnow.info/about/>. This service provides 24/7 live, online Internet chat reference assistance for all residents of Maryland and students in all educational institutions in Maryland. Average sessions last 15 to 20 minutes, and the patron can elect to receive a transcript of the entire reference interaction via e-mail.
- *SVC Redwings Virtual Reference Service* <library.skagit.edu/FAQvrs.html>. Skagit Valley College (WA) hosts this virtual reference service, which is also available to students in Skagit High Schools. Reference questions may be answered via e-mail, or they may be answered real-time, online, or with a library media specialist using chat and co-browsing software.
- *IM A Librarian: Alexandrian Public Library*, Mt. Vernon, IN <www.apl.lib.in.us/im.html>. The Alexandrian Public Library encourages students to Instant Message A Librarian for reference or homework help, using AIM, Yahoo, or MSN Messenger, Monday through Thursday, from 3 p.m.

to 7 p.m. (Advice from Aaron Schmidt, in his "The Young and The Wireless" *School Library Journal* article: "IM is a necessity…If e-mail is the only electronic format you use to communicate with adolescents, your library is at risk of being seen as antiquated" (45).

Conclusion

As we develop our school library media Web pages to provide that virtual library presence for our patrons, we must keep in mind our role as educators and teachers of information literacy. We should include elements and activities that will facilitate students' access, evaluation, and use of information when we are not physically present to guide them. Curriculum support, information literacy instruction, reading promotion, and provision of virtual reference services are vital components of the virtual library.

Exemplary Web Pages for Learning and Teaching

(Selected for the excellent Web page elements which evidence collaboration and support curriculum, learning, and teaching)

- *John Newbery Elementary Library Media Center,* Wenatchee WA <nb.wsd.wednet.edu/lmc/lmc_index.html>. Includes Library Catalogs, Information Databases, Reading Resources, Teacher Resources, Research Resources, Internet Search Tools, and Library Information.

Figure 3.3: John Newbery Elementary Library Media Center Web page. Reprinted with permission from Jeanne Barnes, John Newbery Elementary School, Teacher-Librarian.

- *Thomas Dale High School School Library Media Center,* Chester, VA <chesterfield.k12.va.us/Schools/Dale_HS/library/Virtlib/media.htm>. A comprehensive site, features links to the OPAC, Subscription Databases, Internet Search Engines, A Road Map to Research, Works Cited, Rubrics, Spotlight on Reading, Online Pathfinders, Resources for Staff, Resources for Parents, Virtual Reference Desk, Newspapers, and County Resources.

- *Springfield Township High School Library*, Erdenheim, PA <mciu.org/~spjvweb/>. Attractive and user-friendly, this site features the Reference Desk, Online Lessons, Catalogs and Databases, Links for Teachers, Links for Students, College and Career, Librarian Stuff, Our District, and Pathfinders.

Figure 3.4: Springfield Township High School Library Web page. Reprinted with permission from Joyce Kasman Valenza, Springfield Township High School, Library Information Specialist.

Chapter 3: Learning and Teaching

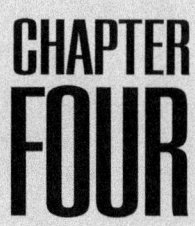

CHAPTER FOUR

Program Administration
Steps to Implementing a Virtual Library

> **From**
> ***Information Power: Building Partnerships for Learning, Chapter 6: Program Administration . . .***
>
> "Principle 1: The library media program supports the mission, goals, objectives, and continuous improvement of the school.
>
> Principle 6: Ongoing assessment for improvement is essential to the vitality of an effective library media program.
>
> Principle 9: Clear communication of the mission, goals, functions, and impact of the library media program is necessary to the effectiveness of the program.
>
> Principle 10: Effective management of human, financial, and physical resources undergirds a strong library media program" (100).

Reprinted with permission from the American Library Association and American Association of School Librarians.

The four principles noted above from Chapter 6 in *Information Power: Building Partnerships for Learning* are certainly addressed as your library goes virtual. A library media program that supports the curriculum of the school virtually through information literacy instruction and access to electronic resources and collaboratively developed pathfinders "supports the mission, goals, objectives, and continuous improvement of the school." And what better way than with your virtual library presence to increase your program's effectiveness by clearly communicating the mission, goals, functions, and impact of the library media program? The school library media Web page provides the perfect place to present your library's mission and goals for all to see. It offers the perfect venue to provide information about upcoming library events (book fairs, reading promotions, and others) as well as showcasing past happenings (how you celebrated Read Across America Day, winning teams from the Battle of the Books contests, and the lunchtime open mike poetry celebration). It also allows you to point patrons to the results of the library impact studies conducted by Keith Curry Lance, Ross Todd, Donna Baumbach, and others, results which show that strong library media programs positively impact student learning (available online at <www.lrs.org/impact.asp>).

Chapters 2 and 3 presented suggestions for information that you might consider including on your library Web page. This chapter addresses issues concerning the administration of your page. As noted in Principle 10 on page 65, effective management of resources is key, and, in Principle 6, continuous assessment for improvement is essential. Here in Chapter 4 we discuss conducting a needs analysis for your library Web page, considerations for virtual collection development, attention to policies that affect your page, marketing for your virtual library, and evaluation of the virtual library.

Needs Analysis for Virtual Content and Services

As you build or redesign your library Web page to meet the needs of your users, a needs assessment is in order. Questions to ask include the following:

- What is the purpose of your Web page?
    - Curriculum support such as pathfinders?

- Connection to quality resources?
- Information literacy instruction and guidance?
- Readers' advisory services?
- Public relations, visibility, advocacy?
- Exactly who will use your Web page, and what type of information does each need?
  - Students?
  - Teachers?
  - Administrators?
  - Parents?
- What services will you need to provide?
  - Tutorials for information seeking?
  - Interactive citation builders?
  - Virtual reference service?

You, as the library media specialist, have knowledge of your collection and your patrons. You have a good idea of where the gaps are and what content and services are needed in electronic format. It is important to have input from your stakeholders as well, however, as you develop the virtual library. How should you undertake getting this input?

One possible method is a survey. Prepare surveys for your teachers, your students, administrators, and parents. The survey could be of the pen-and-paper type, or it could be Web-based, depending on the age and technological access level of your survey participants. If you prefer to use a Web-based survey, consider free/inexpensive survey options such as SurveyMonkey <www.surveymonkey.com>, QuestionPro <www.questionpro.com>, or Zoomerang <www.zoomerang.com>. Collect your data and then analyze it for patterns of responses.

Another possible method to conduct a needs assessment is to use focus groups. Gather a small group of one type of patron together, perhaps students, with a moderator for a somewhat structured discussion about the content and services needed on the library Web page. Then gather another small group together, perhaps teachers. Record the discussions. Still another option is one-on-one interviews with your patrons. Ask them what they need and want and record their answers.

In her doctoral research, Joyce Valenza asked "open-ended text questions . . . of more than 1,200 seniors in 14 high schools with virtual libraries representing best practice" (*Teens and Virtual*). To the question concerning "how their librarian could improve the site," some of the answers she received follow:

Descriptions/Annotations (Frequently requested!): 'Maybe have a synopsis beneath each category to show what it is used for in case we forget.' 'Describe what each search tool is best for.' 'Clearer labeling.'
Teacher/Project Links (They get our connections and partnerships.): 'Direct links to teachers' sites.' 'More of what the teachers go over in class to make sure we understand.'
Databases (They valued these!): 'Greater variety of databases.' 'More programs like Gale.' 'More contemporary databases.' 'Databases with scanned in books.' 'More subscriptions.'
Book Stuff (A surprising number of responses requested more resources relating to books.): 'Include the reading suggestion lists in the library on the page.' 'Organized book lists by genre or author.' 'Link to the OPAC.' 'Book of the month, trivia on books?' (*Teens and Virtual*)

If you ask, they will tell you. Conducting a needs assessment will allow you to develop a virtual library that meets the information needs of your patrons.

Collection Development Considerations

As defined by Evans in his fourth edition of *Developing Library and Information Center Collections Development,* "the goal, for both collection management and information resource management, is to provide accurate information in a timely and cost-effective manner to all members of the service community" (20). Once you have conducted the analysis and determined the needs of your service community, you must select resources that meet the information needs of your patrons and then make those resources available. Although this is your Web page and the information is in electronic format, you want to follow the selection criteria set forth in your collection development policy manual. After all, you are *developing* your virtual *collection*. If you do not have criteria in your policy manual to cover virtual resources—databases, ebooks, and Web sites—now would be a good time to add them.

In addition to the traditionally applied criteria of purpose, audience, authority, accuracy, arrangement, scope, currency, and cost for electronic formats, you will also want to consider accessibility, ease of use, appropriateness for delivery of the content, and any special features. Consider interfaces; consider ease of navigation; consider user-friendliness. Evans notes, "the issue of selection and collection building will remain an important function in whatever environment technology brings" (25).

Attention to Policies
District Policies Related to Web Page Content

Beyond policies related to selection of content for the virtual library, policies are in place at the district, school, and library levels that you will need to consider. One district level policy addresses privacy. With parental permission, most school districts allow student digital photos to be posted on the Web. When student photos are posted, however, there should be no identifying information. You may be allowed to use first names, or the policy may require that no names whatsoever be posted. As Deb Logan and Cynthia Beuselinick note in *K-12 Web Pages: Planning & Publishing Excellent School Web Sites,* "most schools have fairly strict guidelines and policies surrounding the publishing of personal information and photographs on the school Web site" (40). If you plan to use student photos, be sure that you know district policy in this area.

Another district level policy addresses copyright. If you place copyrighted work on the Web page (text or image), be sure that you have written permission to do so. Remember that any work recorded in tangible format is copyrighted upon creation. This includes all student work (creative writing, art work, photography). If you feature student work on the Web page, you must have written permission not only from the student, but also, since the student is a minor, from the student's parents. If the student work includes multimedia components, you will want to be sure that *Fair Use Guidelines for Educational Multimedia* have been observed (information available from <www.utsystem.edu/ogc/intellectualproperty/ccmcguid.htm>).

Another key area related to copyright is licensing agreements. As you provide access to subscription databases, be absolutely sure that you do not violate licensing agreements. You will want to work with your school or district level technology personnel to provide appropriate access to resources, both within the school walls and from home, without infringing upon your licensing agreements. If student access from home requires login and passwords, *do not* give login and password information on the Web page itself. Find another way to keep that information readily available in students' hands, for example, on bookmarks, in student handbooks or agenda books, or newsletters sent home to parents. The objective is to provide legitimate users with as easy access as possible to subscription databases while, at the same time, abiding by licensing agreements.

District Policies Related to Web Page Services

Another area to which you must pay careful attention is district or school policy regarding electronic communication such as e-mail, chatting, and blogging. Policies vary greatly as to what is supported, what is allowed, and what is prohibited. As you develop your Web page, you must work within the policies in place in your district.

> E-mail: Policies range from "staff only" having school e-mail accounts and access to e-mail on school computers to the opposite end of the spectrum with student school e-mail accounts. For an example of school-sponsored student e-mail accounts, take a look at the *4Jnet Guidelines* from Eugene (OR) School District 4J, a school district which provides e-mail accounts for its high school and middle school, and in some cases, elementary school, students (available from <www.4j.lane.edu/4jnet/4jnetguidelines.html>).
>
> Chatting: Many district acceptable use policies prohibit all chat rooms and instant messaging; some actually block instant messaging sites and software. On the other hand, some school districts such as Chicago (IL) Public Schools allow chatting for educational but not personal use. They define as unacceptable: "Using Internet tools such as discussion boards, chat rooms, and instant messaging for personal rather than educational purposes" (*Chicago Public Schools*).

Blogging: Some school districts prohibit blogging, while others encourage it. For an example of a school district that encourages blogging, visit Goochland County (VA) Public Schools where, in April 2006, "teachers are maintaining Weblogs to let parents and students know what's going on in classes—and over 90% of parents like reading them!" (*Goochland County*). (<www.glnd.k12.va.us/podcasts/blogs.shtml>) At Hunterdon Central Regional High School in New Jersey, Weblogs are being used as an instructional tool, "a constructivist learning tool that allows them [educators] to expand their curricula and engage students in meaningful, experiential learning . . . to foster communication and collaboration among teachers, students, parents and community members" (*Weblog Uses*). Prominent on the Hunterdon Central Instructional Media Center page is a blog.

As demonstrated through these few examples, policies vary greatly. Within the guidelines and parameters set by your district and school, you will need to address the concept of virtual reference service. Will you provide reference assistance via e-mail? Will you provide reference assistance via instant messaging? Will you include a blog on your library Web site? If so, will students and others (teachers? parents?) be able to respond to postings on your blog, or will they merely read your posts? Decisions in regard to each of these questions have implications for training, staffing, and workload. If you plan to blog or to provide virtual reference assistance via e-mail or chat, time issues are involved.

Library Policies Regarding Virtual Reference Service
E-mail:

- Will you include an e-mail virtual reference service on your school library Web page?
- If so, will you take questions during the school day?
    - Afternoons?
    - Evenings?

- What will be your guaranteed response time?
    - Twenty-four hours?
    - Forty-eight hours?
    - Monday through Friday?
- Will you take questions from anyone who happens to submit?
    - From students in your school district?
    - From students in your school?

In her article, "Analyzing E-Mail Reference Service in a Museum Library: The Experience of Colonial Williamsburg's John D. Rockefeller, Jr. Library," Juleigh Clark notes that "a comparison of questions answered during the first quarter of 1999 to the first quarter of 2000 showed that e-mail requests increased by 166 percent. As you might imagine, this success both scared and elated the staff" (10-11). If you decide to offer e-mail reference service, you will want to have clear policies in place and clear procedures spelled out. Typical policies seem to be a provision of the service for students currently enrolled in your school with questions answered within 24 hours or the next business day: Questions are both submitted and answered via e-mail. Be sure that you collect data regarding the number of questions submitted and the amount of time spent answering these questions. Data gathered here can demonstrate how your virtual library supports student research and learning.

>Instant messaging: According to Fredericksen, Cummings, and Ursin, as reported in *The Virtual Reference Experience: Integrating Theory Into Practice*, "many libraries are taking advantage of synchronous tools that allow for online, real-time and interactive chat with users, and which also may include graphical co-browsing or 'follow-me' features" (44). Again, if you plan to offer real-time virtual reference assistance, there are questions to answer:

- Will you take questions during the school day?
    - In the afternoons?
    - Evenings?
    - Monday through Friday?

- On weekends? (Perhaps this is a question to ask your students in the needs analysis? "If instant messaging reference were to be available, when would you be most likely to use it?")
- Will you take questions from anyone who happens to submit?
  - From students in your school district?
  - From students in your school?
- Will you use one of the commercially available instant messaging services such as AOL Instant Messenger, Yahoo Messenger, or MSN Messenger?
- Or, will you utilize a more elaborate software package that allows collaborative browsing?

While e-mail reference service requires you to check an account and respond within a designated time, instant messaging reference service requires a different type of commitment, real-time. Again, clear policies and procedures must be in place. ALA's Reference and User Services Association's *Guidelines for Implementing and Maintaining Virtual Reference Services* are very helpful in establishing these policies and procedures (available online at <www.ala.org/ala/rusa/rusaprotools/referenceguide/virtrefguidelines.htm>).

Training

If you plan to include a virtual reference service element on your library Web page, you will still conduct a reference interview of sorts, but it will be in virtual format. ALA's Reference and User Services Association provides *Guidelines for Behavioral Performance of Reference and Information Service Providers*, updated in 2004. "The revised Guidelines reflect the understanding that while in-person and remote reference interviews share some points in common, each also has its own peculiar characteristics that need to be addressed separately in the formation of standard guidelines" (American Library Association *Guidelines for Behavioral*). This document sets forth guidelines for reference service in the areas of "Approachability," "Interest," "Listening/Inquiring," "Searching," and "Follow Up" for the categories of "General," "In Person," and, then, "Remote."

Under "Interest," for example, "General" guidelines include "Focuses attention on the patrons" and the "Remote" guidelines elaborate "Maintains or re-establishes 'word contact' with the patron in text-based environments by sending written or prepared prompts, etc., to convey interest in the patron's question." Under "Searching," "General" suggests "Finds out what patrons have already tried, and encourages patrons to contribute ideas" and "Remote" states "Uses appropriate technology (such as co-browsing, scanning, faxing, etc.) to help guide patrons through library resources, when possible." With "Follow-up," "General," "Asks patrons if their questions have been completely answered," and "Remote" "Suggests that the patrons visit or call the library when appropriate." If you plan to provide virtual reference service, you should review these helpful guidelines in their entirety (available at <www.ala.org/ala/rusa/rusaprotools/reference guide/guidelinesbehavioral.htm>).

Buff Hirko and Mary Bucher Ross present a checklist of 14 "core competencies: knowledge, skills, and aptitudes needed for virtual reference" in their book, *Virtual Reference Training: The Complete Guide to Providing Anytime Anywhere Answers.* If you are considering providing virtual reference service, how would you rate yourself on these?

1. Ability to derive professional satisfaction from virtual reference transactions
2. Keyboarding proficiency
3. Communication skills and etiquette for chat, e-mail, and other online interactions
4. Ability to conduct an effective reference transaction in online environments, including the creation and use of pre-scripted messages
5. Internet searching skills, in particular the ability to choose the best starting points for online searches
6. Ability to effectively search and demonstrate searching of library databases
7. Knowledge of licensing restrictions connected with the use of library databases
8. Ability to assist online users in applying critical thinking skills in locating, using, and evaluating information

9. Ability to effectively conduct a collaborative browsing session with a patron
10. Evaluation of online reference transactions and identification of improvement strategies
11. Multitasking and managing multiple windows; effective use of Windows keyboard commands and shortcuts
12. Technical troubleshooting skills and ability to explain technical problems to facilitate diagnosis and solution
13. Ability to create and apply reference transaction policies in an online environment (e.g., scope of service, time limits, obscene callers, harassment)
14. Commitment to continuous learning and motivation to improve skills in all areas of reference services. (10-11)

Workload

If you implement virtual reference service, you need to be sure that you have the support of your administration. You also need to collect data regarding usage. This data can provide evidence of the library program supporting the instructional program of the school beyond the walls of the library and beyond the regular school day; it can also be valuable when lobbying for additional staff to meet student instructional needs. If you build it, they will come . . . with questions. Imagine the evidence that you can provide of meeting students at the point of need—online—where they are!

If all of this is too much for you and you have no intention of offering virtual reference services via e-mail or instant messaging, consider placing a link on your library Web page to the Virtual Reference Desk AskA+ Locator, <www.vrd.org/locator/subject.shtml>. This site, organized by subject, provides a list of AskA Services resources.

Marketing for the Virtual Library

Your school library Web page—if you build it, they will come—but how will they know it is there? You will put tremendous effort and energy into creating your school library Web page, and you will know what wonderful resources and services it provides for your students, teachers, administrators, and parents. How will your patrons know that it exists? You will have to tell them. And remember, "people generally remember 10% of what they read, 20% of what they hear, 30% of what they see, and 50% of what they see and hear" (Lipow 183). What are some strategies or techniques that you might use to market your library Web page? We will examine on-paper marketing possibilities, in-person possibilities, promotional item possibilities, and virtual possibilities.

On-Paper Possibilities
- Set a goal to put the URL for the library Web page on every piece of paper that leaves your library.
- When you unveil your page, have an article in the local newspaper alerting parents to its availability.
- If you send a library newsletter home to parents, feature the library Web page (complete with screen shot to catch attention) in a prominent article. In subsequent issues, load the URL as part of the footer on every page of the newsletter. Do likewise if you distribute a library newsletter to your faculty and staff.
- Include information about the library Web page on brochures that you develop for parents or for teachers.
- Note the library Web page URL on bookmarks along with other information about the library. You might work with the art teacher to develop a contest for bookmark design.
- As you prepare handouts for classes coming into the library, include the URL on every page of every handout.
- Set up a display or bulletin board that features and explains the library Web page. Use screen shots to show the various options and to showcase the information and services found there.
- Include the URL on your business cards.
- If your school special orders teacher planning books or student agenda books, work with your administration to have the URL for the library Web page prominently displayed in these items.

In-Person Possibilities

- Set a goal to share your library Web page with every group with which you meet or work.
- As you work with classes, demonstrate areas of the library Web page that are applicable to that particular assignment or information need.
- Unveil your library Web page at a faculty meeting. You might even celebrate it with refreshments, as food and drink are certainly positive public relations strategies with faculty members.
- Offer workshops and in-services to demonstrate use of the various portions of your Web page such as access to subscription databases or use of the virtual reference services provided.
- For back-to-school day or parents' open house, set up a kiosk in the hallway with a PowerPoint presentation promoting and explaining use of the library Web page.
- Volunteer to speak at a Parent-Teacher Association meeting to show and tell the Web page.
- If you have voice mail, leave the URL and a reminder to "check the library Web page for all your information needs" at the end of your voice mail message.
- If your school does a student-run morning TV news show, have students promote use of the page there for school assignments as well as for general information purposes.
- If your school has an electronic running message board, be sure the library and its Web page are in the loop.

Promotional Item Possibilities

- If you have funds available, consider pencils, pens, buttons, or even T-shirts sporting the URL.
- If you are in an elementary school and provide plastic bags for students to safely transport books back and forth, consider having the URL printed on the plastic bags.
- Notepads, refrigerator magnets, and post-it notes imprinted with the URL are relatively inexpensive methods by which to share the library Web page with your teachers.

Virtual Possibilities
- Set a goal to promote use of your library Web page through every virtual means readily available to you.
- Notify your faculty and staff of the availability of the new or redesigned library Web page via e-mail and provide the URL.
- If you distribute an electronic newsletter to faculty or parents, feature the library Web page in an article and provide the URL.
- Be sure that a link to the library Web page is prominent and easily-located on the school's homepage.
- Encourage teachers to link to the library Web page when they set up their own Web pages or blogs.
- Include the library Web page URL in your e-mail signature file.
- Make the library Web page the default homepage on all library computers. If it is within your power, make it the default homepage on all computers in the school's computer labs or on all classroom computers within the school.

If you build it, they will come, if they know it is there. Joyce Valenza reports on her blog: "What I am discovering is that effective school library websites are hybrid experiences: most effective when enhanced with face-to-face instruction and supported by faculty endorsement and whole-school programs" (*Interface*). This implies not only that we must build excellent school library Web sites, but also that we must promote their usage and market their potential. And if we do, usage should rise. In his February 2002 Chat Room column in *School Library Journal*, Walter Minkel describes the situation at Inter-Lakes Junior-Senior High School where Eileen Culkin is the library media specialist:

"Things changed, however, after Culkin built a Web site for her library and promoted it to students and teachers as often as she could. Students' research habits have shifted. Before, students went straight to Yahoo! to do their research, ignoring the subscription databases such as ProQuest and Science Facts on File. Now the portal serves as an indispensable research tool to students.

How did she alter teachers' and students' perceptions? Whenever she demonstrated how to research an assignment effectively, she always started from the library site. She convinced several popular teachers to require using it on important assignments. She was quietly stubborn. 'It was a battle to get them to use the Web page,' she says, 'and I convinced them individually.' Now that there's a cart of Apple iBook laptops moving around the school, students are doing more research away from the library. Since she's assembled her subscription databases and recommended sites on the Web page, students both at home and at school are logging into those resources more often" (37).

Evaluation of the Virtual Library

You have completed your needs analysis, developed your virtual library collection, have all policies and procedures in place regarding the library Web page in place, and have marketed the page. Traffic is heavy, and the hit counter you embedded tells you that usage is high. Can you sit back and relax? Not quite yet . . . your next step is to evaluate the page and look for areas to fine-tune. Of course, as you developed the page, you utilized good Web design (see Chapter 5, Technological Aspects), but you still need to check and evaluate now that it is up and running.

Evaluation Criteria

Numerous Web site evaluation criteria and checklists are available. You might want to evaluate your site based on the selection criteria that the International Association of School Librarians uses to select winners of the IASL Concord School Library Web Page Award, which include:

" • Relevance of the page/site to the goals and objectives of the school library;
- Visual appeal, including layout, choice of images, type face, and style;
- Organization of information on the page/site;
- Quality of the writing and use of language (and proof-reading);
- Ease of use of the page/site and navigational features;
- Educational, information, entertainment, or public relations value of the page/site;
- Appropriateness for the needs of users;

- Currency, evidence of update policy, and the provision of current information or links;
- Technical quality (note that this is interpreted as the appropriate use of technology, not necessarily leading-edge technology);
- Value of the page/site as a model for other school libraries and/or school librarians" (*IASL/Concord School Library*)

Or, you might want to use the criteria and explanations that Annette Lamb sets forth under *Information Architecture for the Web: Web Development for Schools and Libraries—Website Evaluation*. She presents these "as a guide as you develop your own professional website review" and offers numerous helpful questions (available at <eduscapes.com/arch/arch7.html>) to be answered under each of these criteria:

- Overall impressions
- Content aspects
- Design aspects
- Navigation aspects
- Technical and usability aspects
- Maintenance aspects
- Content enhancements

Or, a third option for evaluation would be to use the standard basic five criteria for evaluating Web pages: accuracy, authority, currency, objectivity, and coverage (*Five Criteria*) to see how well your page measures up. If none of these options appeals to you, visit Kathy Schrock's *Guide for Educators* and choose one of the excellent critical evaluation checklists offered on her *Critical Evaluation Surveys and Resources* page at <school.discovery.com/schrockguide/eval.html>.

Feedback from Users

You also want to get feedback from your users concerning the library Web site's functionality, its content, and the services it provides. If you provide virtual reference service via e-mail, chat, or instant messaging, you want to evaluate these services according to criteria such as promptness, accuracy, clarity, and comprehensiveness (Jaeger

209). Even if you do not provide virtual reference service, however, you want to evaluate the library Web site itself to determine how well it is "meeting the information needs of specific patron groups, providing access to specific types of resources, [and achieving] patron satisfaction" (Pomerantz 38). In her book *The Virtual Reference Librarian' Handbook*, Anne Grodzins Lipow offers several methods by which to gather this data. The first method that she suggests is to conduct usability studies, observing users as they use the Web site in as natural a setting as possible and as they use it on your terms.

Observing users as naturally as possible: Lipow suggests that you recruit a user for a certain amount of time and observe her as she uses the library Web page, asking her to think aloud as she searches. Listen to what she says she is searching for, paying careful attention to how her terminology differs from what you have used on the page. Take notes, and with her permission, record what she says. Repeat this with several users and several different types of users—students, teachers, parents, and administrators. You are trying to view and use the library Web page through their eyes (119).

Observing users on your terms: Here Lipow suggests that you follow the same steps as above, except this time you have the user search a topic or a question that you have developed. Compare what the patron does and says to what you thought he would do or say (120). With these two studies, you can determine the usability of your site and make any needed adjustments.

Another method that Lipow suggests is to provide a "post-transaction evaluation form . . . an easy-to-use, *short* evaluation form. The form should fit within the boundaries of one screen and should encourage users to tell what they liked and didn't like about using your service" (119). Sample questions that might be included are as follows:

- Have you used this library Web page before?   Yes   No
- Did you use it for
    - A class assignment
    - Information you wanted to look up
    - Help in finding a book to read
    - Asking the librarian for help
    - Other (please explain)

- How helpful was this library Web page for you?
    - Very helpful   Helpful   Not Helpful
- Any suggestions for improving this library Web page?

A third evaluation method that Lipow suggests is focus group meetings with users to discuss what they like and do not like about the library Web page, how it helps them, and suggestions that they have for change or for improvement.

You should choose a method to evaluate your library Web page that works for you in your library in your school. It does not matter which method you choose. It does matter that you choose one and use it. You need evaluative data not only to further develop and improve your page but also to document the virtual service that you are providing for your users.

Conclusion

To effectively develop, implement, and evaluate a virtual library requires sound practice in program administration. It requires careful management of human, financial, and physical resources; clear communication of the library media program's mission, goals, and function; and ongoing assessment and evaluation for continuous improvement. The virtual library contributes to the needed information access and delivery and to the learning and teaching that occurs in your school because it is carefully and thoughtfully developed and administered.

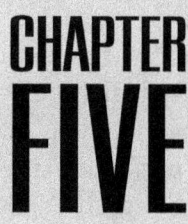

Technological Aspects

From
Information Power: Building Partnerships for Learning . . .

". . . the school library media specialist uses technology from the perspective of the technologist, integrating people, learning, and the tools of technology. Using the technologist's concepts and tools, the school library media specialist analyzes a need, designs a way to meet it, tests the design, and evaluates and revises it" (54-55).

Reprinted with permission from the American Library Association and American Association of School Librarians.

This chapter addresses the technological aspects of creating your virtual library. We will explore the larger technological context in which you will work (your school and school district), discuss principles of good Web design, and address site accessibility issues. Suggestion: Before you begin to construct or reconstruct your Web site, spend a good bit of time online browsing and viewing school library Web sites. Make specific notes in two columns: what you like and what you simply cannot stand. Use these notes and keep these thoughts in mind as you begin to create your virtual library. The purpose of this chapter is to help you get started to create or revitalize your school library Web page.

Larger School Technology Context

As you begin to design your school library Web page, there are key questions to ask to determine how your page fits into the larger school picture. You want to find out what are the policies and where is the power.

- Is it permissible for you to design your school library Web page, or must another person (such as the school Webmaster or the school technology coordinator) do this with the content that you provide?
- If it is permissible for you to create your page, is a certain layout or design required? Are there templates that you must follow, either created in-house or purchased commercially? Good Web design suggests consistency across a site, so you may be required to follow a certain layout that is consistent with your school's site or even your school district's site. If this is not the case and you are free to design as you like, remember to practice the "consistency rule" from page to page within your library Web site.
- Does your school or school district require the use of a certain Web development software package, perhaps Macromedia's *Dreamweaver* or Microsoft's *FrontPage*? If not, consider one of the quality free Web design programs available such as *Nvu* (available for download from <www.nvu.com>) or *Quanta Plus* (available for download

from <quanta.kdewebdev.org/>) or *Netscape Composer* (available from <wp.netscape.com/communicator/composer/v4.0/index.html>).
- How will the files for your Web page be uploaded to the Web server? As Logan and Beuselinck note in *K-12 Web Pages: Planning & Publishing Excellent School Sites*, "Some school districts will do all the uploading for their schools. This step increases the safety of the server and can help with maintaining quality control and consistency. It does, however, create an enormous workload and rob schools of their ability to make quick changes to their own Web sites. Other schools or districts permit numerous people to upload school pages" (70).
- Which brings us to the next question ... How frequently will you be able to update your page? Your ability to upload files impacts the currency of the material you can put on your site. If you have the capability to update your library Web page as needed, you can certainly plan on updating the site more often than you could if you were required to send the files to a Webmaster for uploading.

Once you have the answers to these basic questions, you are ready to begin designing your library Web site.

Web Design
Planning
It is absolutely essential that you have a plan, a structure, for your library Web site. James Herring, author of *Internet Information Skills: A Guide for Teachers and Librarians*, suggests the use of a storyboard to "outline [the] site design on paper . . . so that you can think clearly about structure before actually designing your pages" (116). If you prefer, rather than drawing the site outline on paper, you might use *Inspiration* to brainstorm and outline how your site will be organized. As Herring notes, "Getting the right structure for the school website is the first step towards a logically organized and useable site, so getting the structure of the homepage right is crucial" (117). You should develop a storyboard for your site homepage and then for each internal page of the site as well.

As you design your site, keep your users in the forefront of your mind; the library Web site is for them, not for you. Patrons search for sites that are easy to access, easy to navigate, easy to read, person-to-person, engaging, and frustration-free (Lipow 138-146). Debbie Abilock, in her "Focus on the User" Homepage column in the January/February 2005 issue of *Knowledge Quest*, points out that we frequently use our library terminology on our Web pages, rather than words that users will understand; for example, we use "Database" rather than "Collection of Journal Articles" or "Find Articles" and "OPAC" rather than "Library Catalog" or "Find Books." We must make our site user-friendly and use terminology that patrons understand. Keep these goals in mind as you develop your library Web site.

Layout and Appearance

As you design your site, pay attention to elements of good Web design:

- Appearance: Keep your page uncluttered. Use white space strategically.
- Color: Use a white background with black text. If you wish to use other colors, keep the background light and the text dark.
- Layout: Keep the layout standard and consistent from page to page within your site; include your library's name (and logo, if you have one) on each page.
- Navigation: Make navigation obvious and easy for users by providing a navigation bar in the same location on each page. Be sure that the user can always return easily and directly to the homepage from anywhere within the site.
- Content:
  - Make your headings and subheadings more visible by indenting the content.
  - Keep paragraphs short, four sentences or less, organizing text into chunks.
  - Bullet lists of more than two items.
  - Use fonts wisely to direct the readers' eyes to key information. If the information is such that you want students to skim it, use larger font size.

- Create eye magnets. To draw readers' attention to key information on page, either bold key text or use an appropriate graphic. If it is information that should be carefully read, for example, tips on which database to choose, bold the heading (database title) to attract the students' attention, then follow with the information to be read (explanation) in the same font size.
- Links: When you provide links, link to the specific information needed, not to an "outer" page, which then requires your users to perform additional mouse clicks.
- Graphics: Use generic clip art sparingly, if at all.
    - Be sure that your graphics are appropriate for the content and that they have a purpose.
    - Be conscious of download time. (A good rule of thumb is no digital photo larger than 35K.) Consider download time as you use multimedia files as well.
    - Place an ALT tag on each graphic to accommodate visually challenged users.
    - Avoid animated GIFs and blinking icons. (These not only can be distracting but also have been shown to trigger seizures.)
- Basic Information: Give each page of the site a clear title, and make it obvious who created the site, when it was created, and when it was last updated. Include contact information, at least an e-mail address.
- Grammar and spelling: Check and double-check your grammar, spelling, capitalization, and punctuation. Remember that your library Web page is your library's presence outside the library and school walls. Make sure that it puts forth the most positive and professional image possible (Abilock 6-7; Herring 122; Lipow 92-94; Minkel *Remaking* 46-49; Warlick *Building* 14-15).

Usability

What do we know specifically about Web site usability for children? Dr. Jakob Nielsen studied elementary age children (ages six to 12) and reported a summary of his findings in his April 14, 2002, Alertbox column. Dr. Nielsen reported that children locate information best on simple, well-designed Web sites. They do not have the patience or the knowledge (contrary to popular belief) to work around usability problems such as unclear navigation or complicated wording. They do not like slow downloads and frequently are using older, hand-me-down computers in both home and school settings, and they often give up and go to another site if the computer "takes too long" or if they receive an error message or a broken link. They are "keenly aware of their age and differentiate sharply between material that is appropriate for them and material for older or younger kids, however close in age they may be" (3).

In general children enjoyed animation and sound effects, were willing to sweep the page to find clickable areas, did not like to scroll down past one screen for information, liked geographic navigation metaphors that allowed them to enter rooms or move across maps, and were willing to read a paragraph or so of instructions in order to complete an activity or play a new game. If you are designing a site for elementary school students, you might consider Nielsen's full report of usability guidelines for designing Web sites for children available from <www.nngroup.com/reports/kids/>.

Dr. Nielsen also conducted a Web site usability study for teenagers (ages 13 through 17) and reported his findings in his Jan. 31, 2005, Alertbox column, summarizing "When using websites, teenagers have a lower success rate than adults and they're also easily bored. To work for teens, websites must be simple—but not childish—and supply plenty of interactive features" (1).

Nielsen determined that teenagers are successful at completing a representative task on a Web site only 55 percent of the time due to their "insufficient reading skills, less sophisticated search strategies, and a dramatically lower patience level" (3). Clean (but not boring) design attracts them, and they prefer visuals and graphics to dense text. Since they prefer to scan, they do not like small font sizes but they are willing to scroll down for information. If you are designing a site for middle or high school students, you might consider Nielsen's full report of usability guidelines for designing Web sites for teenagers available at <www.nngroup.com/reports/teens/>.

Readability

Several eyetracking studies have been done to determine how users approach and read a Web page. In the January/February 2005 issue of *Knowledge Quest*, Debbie Abilock discusses findings from the 2004 Eyetrack III study, a usability study conducted by the Poynter Institute. Studying eye movements of 46 people reading online news accounts, researchers found that "readers enter a Web page in the upper left-hand quadrant, stop and focus, then traverse into the upper right-hand quadrant (perhaps a pattern retained from print reading). Then they continue toward the bottom left, scan the bottom, and end by moving upward along the right edge" (6). This study found that user eye movements roughly followed the shape of a "Z."

In his April 17, 2006, Alertbox column Dr. Jakob Nielsen reports finding an "F" shaped pattern for reading Web content: "eyetracking visualizations show that users often read Web pages in an F-shaped pattern: two horizontal stripes followed by a vertical stripe" (1). Nielsen tracked the eye movements of 232 people as they explored thousands of Web sites. According to his findings, users will read across the topic of your page, move down a short distance and read across the page again, and then vertically scan the content's left side. Nielsen's advice: "users won't read your text thoroughly . . . the first two paragraphs must state the most important information . . . start subheads, paragraphs, and bullet-points with information carrying words" (3).

Accessibility Issues

Our goal as library media specialists is to provide information access and delivery to all our patrons; therefore, as we design our school library Web pages, we must certainly keep accessibility issues in mind. Our patrons may have visual disabilities (such as complete blindness, impaired vision, or color blindness) or auditory disabilities (such as deafness or impaired hearing). They may have physical or motor disabilities (which make it difficult for them to manipulate a mouse or to hold down several keys at one time) or cognitive/language disabilities (which may cause poor spatial reasoning or the inability to read and understand written text) (*Accessibility Guidelines* 1-2).

For basic guidelines to design accessible Web sites and interfaces, visit the U.S. Department of Health and Human Services'

Usability: Accessibility Resources Web site at < www.usability.gov/accessibility/index.html>. This site discusses usability basics, presents methods for designing accessible Web sites, and gives guidelines and checklists for Web design, in addition to numerous links to accessibility resources. For official information regarding Section 508 of the Rehabilitation Act, which requires all federal agencies to make electronic and information technologies accessible to people with disabilities, visit *Section 508: The Road to Accessibility* at <www.section508.gov>.

If you would like to manually test the accessibility of your site, Blowers and Bryan suggest a few simple methods in their book, *Weaving a Library Web: A Guide to Developing Children's Websites.*

- Turn off the graphics to see if you are able to understand and navigate the site without images. (To do this in Internet Explorer, select Tools from the menu bar, then Internet Options, then Advanced. Scroll down and in the Multimedia section, uncheck the option Show pictures. Refresh your screen and then perform your test.)
- Copy your site into Notepad to view the content in the same way that screen reader software will approach it to read it to a person with visual or cognitive disabilities. (To do this, select Edit from your browser menu, Select All, and Copy. Open Notepad and Paste.)
- View your site in black and white to be sure that color is not a critical element in navigation or understanding of the page. Simply print out the pages in black and white and read through them carefully.
- Unplug your mouse to determine if it is still possible to navigate through your site using keyboard commands (Tab, arrow, and Enter keys).

If you would like to actually check your page against Section 508 guidelines and Web Content Accessibility Guidelines (WCAG), you might consider using the following services. *Bobby*, originally a product of CAST, the Center for Applied Special Technology, and now produced and distributed by WebXACT, is a free online service that lets you test single pages of Web content for quality, accessibility, and privacy issues. For each URL that you process through Bobby, you get a full report of potential accessibility problems. *Bobby* from Watchfire is available at <webxact.watchfire.com>. Another free online Web accessibility service is *Cynthia Says*, a product of the Joint Education and Outreach Project of HiSoftware, ICDRI, and the Internet Society and Special Needs Chapter. *Cynthia Says* allows you to test your page for 508 and W3C WCAG (Web Content Accessibility Guidelines) compliance, providing feedback in an easy-to-understand report, immediately returned to the user. *Cynthia Says* is available at <www.cynthiasays.com/>. As we develop our school library Web pages, we must take steps to ensure that they are accessible to all of our patrons, those with and without disabilities.

Testing, Upkeep, and Maintenance

After you have worked hard to design and create your library Web site, making it accessible to all your patrons, you want to have a plan in place to be sure that it remains functional and current. Did you know that your Web page may look different when opened in different browsers? To determine how your page will appear in Microsoft Internet Explorer, Netscape Navigator, Mozilla Firefox, and other commonly used browser software, visit *Browsercam* at <www.browsercam.com>. *Browsercam* allows you to check your site's compatibility in various browsers and various operating systems, showing you screen captures of how your site appears in each.

Did you also know that your Web page may look different on computers set at various screen resolutions? *WebCanopy.com Free Web Tools Screen Size Validator* at <www.webcanopy.com/tools_scrntest.cfm> allows you to choose a screen size to view the layout of your page at various screen resolution sizes, from 640 X 480 to 1,024 X 768. To check for load times for your page on dial-up connection, ISDN, cable, T1, or DSL, consider using *ZDNet Developer Netmechanic HTML Toolbox* at <www.netmechanic.com/cobrands/zd_dev/>. This online service will check up to five pages for free for broken links, download times, and other potential problems and give you an immediate, easy-to-read report.

If you would like to install a counter on your Web page that also provides you with user statistics, check out *StatCounter* at <www.statcounter.com>. The service is free up to 250,000 page loads per month and reasonably priced if you need to upgrade due to heavy traffic. You want to be certain that your site has no broken, non-working links. *W3C Link Checker* at <validator.w3.org/checklink> is a free site that checks anchors and links and reports problems identified. Careful attention to upkeep and maintenance will ensure that visitors are not frustrated by out-dated and broken links.

Conclusion

In this chapter, we have explored the technological context in which you will develop your school library Web page. You need to be cognizant of the technological environment within your school and school district because your library Web page will be one piece of that puzzle, and it should be a good fit. You need to follow the principles of good Web design as you develop your page, planning its structure, focusing on layout and appearance, and keeping in mind findings from recent usability and readability studies. As you develop your school library Web site, you want to make it accessible to all your users, and you want to plan for continued upkeep and maintenance.

CHAPTER SIX

The Larger Learning Community

Where Are We Now?

From

***Information Power: Building Partnerships for Learning, Chapter 7: Connections to the Learning Community* . . .**

"Authentic learning for today's student is not bound by the textbook, the classroom, the library media center, or the school. By linking students with unlimited learning opportunities available throughout the learning community, the school library media program provides a bridge between formal, school-based learning and independent, lifelong learning" (122).

Reprinted with permission from the American Library Association and American Association of School Librarians.

By creating the school library Web page and providing that virtual library presence for patrons, we are able to guide and connect them to resources in the larger learning community. In this chapter we briefly explore several research studies involving school library Web sites. Next we examine the current status of state virtual libraries that provide services for K-12 schools and then look at several virtual schools to discover the kind of library services their students have. We conclude with thoughts and discussion of present and future virtual school libraries.

School Library Media Center Web Pages: 1996-2006

Early exploration of school library Web sites was done by the late Laurel A. Clyde, Professor and Chair of the Library and Information Science Department at the University of Iceland. In 1996, as schools were just beginning to post sites on the World Wide Web, she selected 50 school library Web sites (from Peter Milbury's *Network of School Librarian Web Pages* and Linda Bertland's *School Libraries on the Web*) and performed content analysis to describe what features a then "state-of-the-art" school library Web site included. In 1999 she re-examined the sites and then again in 2002. Of the 50 sites studied in 1996, 32 were still available in 2002. To answer the question of what is "state-of-the-art" for school library Web sites in 2002, she reported,

> On the one hand, there are a few school library Web sites that consist of just one page that has either not been updated for several years, or that has seen only minor changes of wording over the years. These pages enable the school libraries to claim a Web presence; some act as a billboard to advertise the presence of a library on the school Web site; but their usefulness is limited in any other respect. On the other end of the scale, there are a few comparatively large school library Web sites, with more than 40 pages of information and many features designed to meet the needs of users. Most school library Web sites fall somewhere between these two extremes (Clyde 164).
>
> The most sophisticated of the school library Web sites provide information about the school library, collections of evaluated links to Internet resources for library users

(including students, teachers, the library staff, and occasionally parents), a link to the school library OPAC and other useful library catalogues (such as the catalogue of the local public library and/or a local library consortium catalogue), and links to commercial online information services (with access available for teachers and students from home as well as from school) (Clyde 165).

An analysis of the overall development of the pages showed that "between 1996 and 1999 more than half of the school library Web sites became more sophisticated, as indicated by an increased number of pages on the site and/or an increase in the resources made available through the site. More than a third became more sophisticated in terms of graphics and design . . . In the second three-year period (1999-2002), the rate of development slowed somewhat" (165). Clyde's conclusion from her longitudinal study: "there is evidence of an important emerging function for the school library Web site as an electronic information gateway" (166), a connection to the larger learning community.

In spring 2004 Donna J. Baumbach, Professor of Educational Media/Instructional Technology in the College of Education, University of Central Florida, Orlando, studied 100 school library Web pages in the United States randomly selected from the *School-Libraries.net* list. She reported that 70 percent of the sites studied included a link from the school's main Web page. Sixty-seven percent included links to online databases, and 62 percent promoted reading in some fashion (Baumbach 9). Baumbach expressed surprise that 70 percent of these library sites are linked from the school homepage, since "in a random sample of twenty public schools with Web pages in six southeastern states, fewer than 30 percent linked to their libraries from the main page on their school portal" (8) and in a study of Florida schools, "only about 42 percent linked it [the school main page] to the school library media center's Web page or resources" (9). Her explanation of this striking difference is that those library media specialists whose pages are listed on *School-Libraries.net* take a proactive stance within their schools, making it much more likely that a link to their page would appear on the school homepage.

In the June 2005 *School Library Journal,* Sally Brewer, Associate Professor of Library Media and Technology, University of Montana-Missoula, and Peggy Milam, National Board Certified Library Media Specialist at Compton Elementary School in Cobb County, Georgia, reported on "SLJ's Technology Survey: When It Comes to Education, Librarians are Key Players in Bringing Our Schools Into the 21st Century." Responding from 50 states, 1,571 K-12 library media specialists reported on their role in technology in their schools. "Library media specialists are also responsible for resources on the Web. Two-thirds, or a little more than 1,000 respondents, have a library Web site. And approximately 70 percent said that their sites include a Web-based, online public-access catalog, or OPAC; online databases; curricular links; and other resources that students can access 24/7. These same media specialists told us that they designed and created the library site and also maintain it" (51). Of course, we must examine survey respondents here, too. These library media specialists who are so active in developing their library Web sites are library media specialists who took the time to respond to a survey concerning technology. From these studies, it is obvious that in the past 10 years, library media specialists have taken an active role in technology and that school library Web sites have developed greatly to provide access to information resources.

State-Level Virtual Libraries Providing Services for K-12 Schools

As we work to help our students connect to the larger learning community, we must look at state virtual libraries. Virtual libraries provided at the state level offer not only tremendous access to quality information for K-12 students and teachers, but also significant cost savings to individual school libraries. In an explanation about *MARVEL! Maine's Virtual Library,* the budgetary implications are clearly explained. "One example of cost savings is as follows: Maine has 214 schools (public and private) that contain grades 9-12. If one of these schools were to purchase just the EBSCO resources contained in MARVEL!, it would cost that school $16,800. If all of these 214 Maine schools purchased just the EBSCO materials on their own, the total cost would be $3,595,200" (*MARVEL!* 1).

Table 6:1 **State Virtual Library URLs**

State	Library	URL
Alabama	AVL: Alabama Virtual Library	http://www.avl.lib.al.us/
Alaska	SLED	http://sled.alaska.edu/databases/home.html
Arizona		http://www.dlapr.lib.az.us/index.cfm?Collections Programs/DatabasesEtc#databases
Arkansas	Traveler	http://www.asl.lib.ar.us/traveler/index.html
Connecticut	ICONN	http://www.iconn.org
Delaware	DelAWARE	http://www.state.lib.de.us/Collection_Development/ Electronic_Resources/DelAWARE/
Florida	Florida Electronic Library	http://www.flelibrary.org/index.cfm
Georgia	GALILEO	http://www.galileo.usg.edu
Hawaii		http://www.state.hi.us/libraries/hsl/databases.html
Idaho	LiLI	http://www.lili.org/
Illinois	Find It! Illinois!	http://www.finditillinois.org/articles.html
Indiana	INSPIRE	http://www.inspire.net/
Iowa	SILO	http://www.statelibraryofiowa.org/ld/databases
Kansas	KanFind	http://skyways.lib.ks.us/library/databases.html
Kentucky	KY Virtual Library	http://www.kyvl.org/
Louisiana		http://lalibcon.state.lib.la.us/
Maine	MARVEL!	http://libraries.maine.edu/mainedatabases/
Maryland	Sailor	http://www.sailor.lib.md.us/
Massachusetts		http://mblc.state.ma.us/index.php
Michigan	MeL	http://www.mel.org/screens/databasesubjects.html
Minnesota	ELM	http://elm4you.org/
Mississippi	MAGNOLIA	http://library.msstate.edu/magnolia/
Missouri	MOREnet	http://www.more.net/online/
Montana	MLN	http://montanalibraries.org/
Nebraska	NebraskaAccess	http://www.nlc.state.ne.us/nebraskaccess/index.html
Nevada	CLAN	http://www.clan.lib.nv.us/Polaris/
New Hampshire	NHewLINK	http://www.nhewlink.state.nh.us/schools/index.html
New Jersey		http://www.njstatelib.org/Electronic_Resources/ #databases
New Mexico		http://www.stlib.state.nm.us/services_more .php?id=203_0_13_0_M38
New York	NOVEL	http://www.nysl.nysed.gov/library/novel/
North Carolina	WISE OWL	http://www.ncwiseowl.com/
North Dakota	LaND	http://ndsl.lib.state.nd.us/ElectronicResources .html#K12
Ohio	INFOHIO	http://www.infohio.org/
Oklahoma	Digital Prairie	http://www.odl.state.ok.us/prairie/index.htm
Oregon	OSLIS	http://www.oslis.k12.or.us/
Pennsylvania	POWER	http://www.powerlibrary.net/
South Carolina	DISCUS	http://www.scdiscus.org/index.html
South Dakota		http://www.sdstatelibrary.com/
Tennessee	TEL	http://access.gale.com/tel2/
Texas		
Utah	Pioneer	http://pioneer-library.org/
Vermont	VOL	http://www.burnham.lib.vt.us/Vermont%20Online.htm
Virginia	FindItVa	http://www.finditva.com
Washington		http://www.psesd.org/technology/ProQuest/UMI.html
West Virginia		http://librarycommission.lib.wv.us/ebsco/ebsco.htm
Wisconsin	BadgerLink	http://www.badgerlink.net/
Wyoming	GoWYLD	http://gowyld.net/dbases.html

Table 6.1 presents the URL for the virtual libraries available in 46 states. If you, as a library media specialist, have not investigated and made connections with the virtual library in your state, you should do so immediately. For example, Mississippi's MAGNOLIA provides online databases for Mississippi's K-12 public schools, public libraries, community college libraries, and university libraries. It includes products from EBSCOHost, Gale, Grolier, ProQuest, and Wilson.

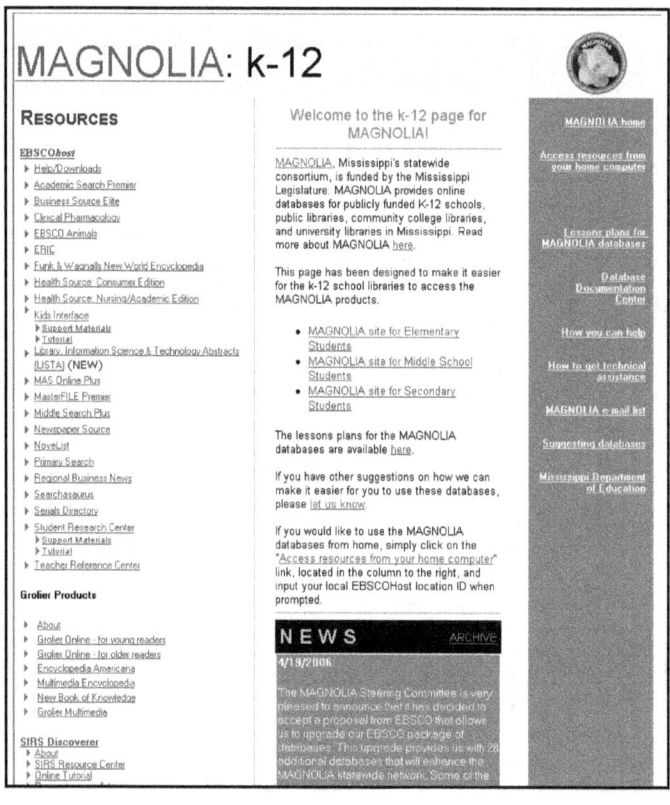

Figure 6.2: MAGNOLIA Web page. Reprinted with permission from Mississippi State University Libraries, Stephen Cunetto, Administrator of Systems.

Maine's MARVEL! offers databases from EBSCOHost and Gale as well as Encyclopaedia Britannica—thousands of magazines, newspapers, and reference books for every library and school in Maine.

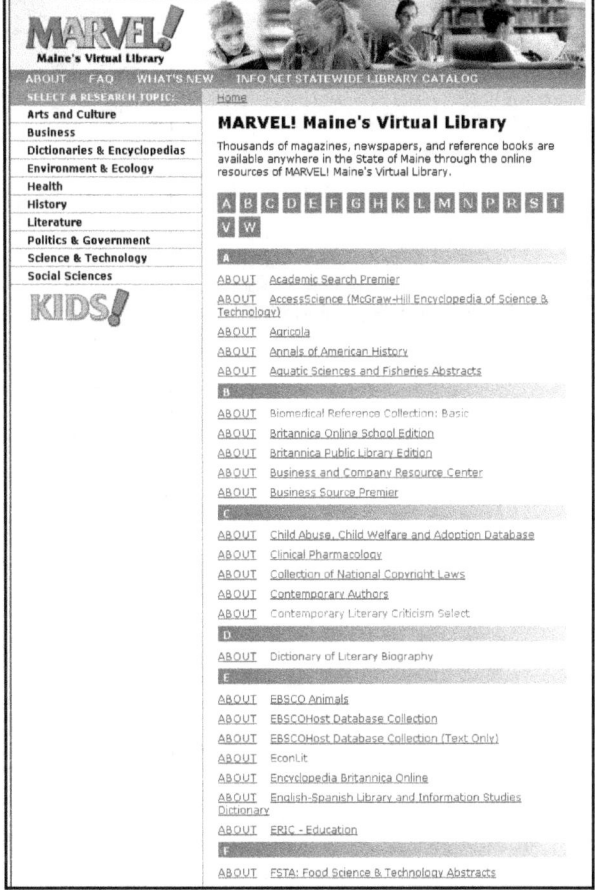

Figure 6.3: MARVEL! Web page. Reprinted with permission from Maine State Library, Bonnie Dwyer, Central Maine Library District Consultant.

Wisconsin's BadgerLink offers access to EBSCOHost, ProQuest, and Gale products, while Minnesota's ELM presents magazine, newspaper, and journal articles, ebooks, and reference sources from EBSCO, Gale, NetLibrary, OCLC, and ProQuest.

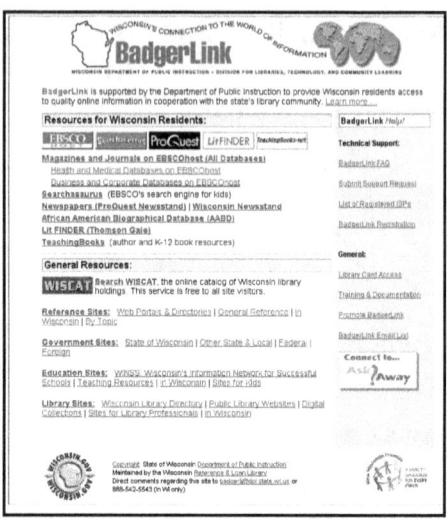

Figure 6.4: BadgerLink Web page. Reprinted with permission from Wisconsin Department of Public Instruction, James Leaver, BadgerLink Coordinator.

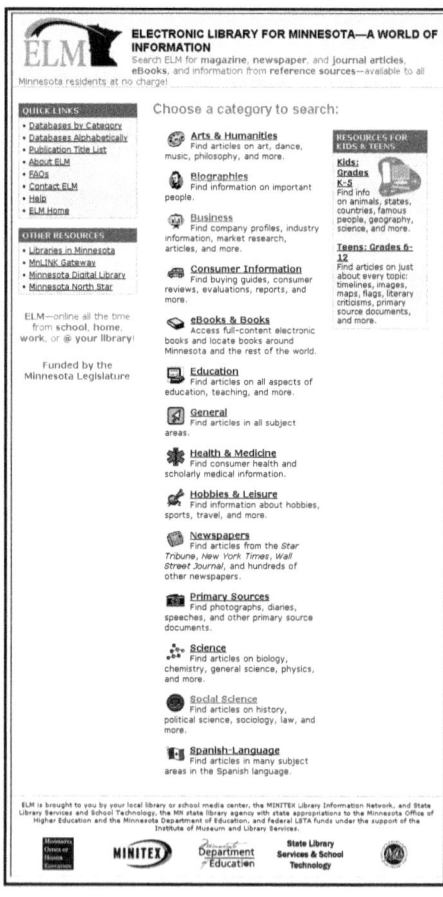

Figure 6.5: ELM Web page. Reprinted with permission from MINITEX Library Information Network, Mary Parker, Associate Director.

100   *Your Library Goes Virtual*

As you construct your school library Web page, be sure that you provide links to these electronic resources available through the state level virtual libraries. It is not sufficient, however, merely to provide links. You must proactively promote and actively train students and teachers to use these resources.

In the Williams, Grimble, and Irwin study, "Teachers' Link to Electronic Resources in the Library Media Center," reported in the 2004 *School Library Media Research Online,* given a list of specific electronic resources (such as BigChalk Elibrary Database, Gale, Opposing Viewpoints), most of the teachers indicated they were 'not familiar' with the databases. The percentage of teachers not familiar with a specific resource ranged from 54 to 83 percent, depending on the database. Resources that received a majority of responses in the 'familiar' or 'very familiar' level were the CHS Web page (99 percent), the Carmel Clay Schools Web page (99 percent), CHS's library catalog (88 percent), and the Internet (99 percent). The teachers' assessment of the value of specific electronic resources was related to their familiarity with them (Williams, Grimble, Irwin 5).

Further investigation of teachers' use of electronic databases showed that if teachers were not familiar with and comfortable with using a database, (a) they did not use it, and (b) they certainly did not recommend it to their students. "Seventy-eight percent of the faculty 'sometimes' or 'often' refer their students to the Internet, 30 percent or more 'never' refer students to specific print reference materials, multimedia resources, and electronic databases" (Williams, Grimble, Irwin 6).

Resources available through state virtual libraries are too powerful to ignore. We, as library media specialists, must feature them on our library Web pages and facilitate their usage with teachers. In an article in the February 2005 *Teacher Librarian,* Mary Ann Bell, Assistant Professor of Library Science at Sam Houston State University in Huntsville, Texas, reports on the status of state-funded electronic resources for K-12 schools in the United States. As Bell conducted her research she found that five states had no access to state level virtual libraries (California, Colorado, Florida, Rhode Island, and Texas). Since that time, Florida has added access to databases through its Sunlink project, and Texas has made inroads in restoring access at regional levels. The concern, however, is that in challenging budgetary times, funding for the electronic databases may be reduced or even lost. Bell advises that we "encourage students and teachers to use the resources regularly . . . emphasizing the importance of turning to them for information rather than 'free surfing' of the Internet" (10). She also suggests that we "advertise database availability and value to parents and community members" (10). What better way to accomplish both of these charges than by highlighting and promoting the use of state level electronic resources on the school library Web page.

Virtual Libraries Serving Virtual K-12 Schools

Thus far, our discussion has centered on providing a school library Web page or virtual presence for your library *in addition to* your physical library space in your school. But what of virtual schools? As more and more states offer virtual courses or virtual schools, what type of library services are available for students who attend these schools? What are the implications for library services?

Many states that offer virtual school courses offer them in conjunction with regular school attendance. Students who wish to accelerate or to take courses not offered on campus at their physical school supplement their traditional coursework with online course offerings. For example, the Virginia Department of Education's Virtual Advanced Placement School provides a variety of college level and foreign language courses for Virginia high school students through distance education from Art History to Human Geography to Micro Economics to Latin III (*Virginia Department of Education*). Similarly, the Kentucky Virtual High School offers core courses, advanced placement courses, and foreign language courses (*Kentucky Virtual High School*). In Louisiana, students use Web and e-mail as well as online and offline resources to participate in Louisiana Virtual School courses. Is the virtual school concept gaining in popularity? Statistics from the Louisiana Virtual School indicate that this is the case:

- Academic year 2000-2001—130 students, 12 courses, 20 schools, nine districts
- Academic year 2004-2005—2,300 students, 30 courses, 175 schools, 60+ districts (*Louisiana Virtual School*).

You, as library media specialist, must be aware of virtual courses offered in your school. If a course were offered physically in your school, you would add resources to your library collection to support the curriculum and instruction of that course. Students enrolled in virtual courses are online already; capitalize on their online behavior. Be sure that the library Web page offers resources that meet their needs. Make sure that it is their information portal to the Web, the first choice resource. The school library Web page may be one element that connects them to their home school.

Another approach to virtual schools can be seen in the Florida Virtual School, "founded in 1997 [as] the country's first state-wide Internet-based public high school. Today FLVS serves middle and high school students with more than 80 courses" (*Florida Virtual School*). Students in FLVS receive virtual library services through Florida's Ask A Librarian, "a free online information service provided by Florida libraries. Real people in real time answer your questions, help you find information, or point you in the right direction to get what you need" (*Ask A Librarian*). Students can submit questions via e-mail 24/7 or receive real time reference assistance from 10 a.m. to 10 p.m., Sunday through Friday, and 10 a.m. to 5 p.m. on Saturday. Virtual school equals virtual library service—making the learning connection.

Virtual Libraries: Present and Future

Our first *Information Power: Guidelines for School Library Media Programs* was published in 1988, challenging us with a mission "to ensure that students and staff are effective users of ideas and information" (American Association of School Librarians 6). Our current set of national guidelines, *Information Power: Building Partnerships of Learning,* was published in 1998. In 2006 I am amazed at the foresight that the writers had. Information literacy standards; our focus on collaboration, leadership, and technology; learning and teaching; information access and delivery; program administration; and attention to the larger community are still critical elements in the school library world. Where will school libraries be 10 years from now? What will be the state of our virtual presence, our school library Web pages? If we know one thing about technology, it is that it will change. As we listen to current discussions of the future of libraries, we hear terms such as Web 2.0, Library 2.0, wikis, podcasting, and

RSS feeds. How much of this will come to pass? How much of it will our K-12 schools embrace?

In February 2006 Michael Stephens posted *The Digitally Re-Shifted School Library: A Conversation with Christopher Harris* on the ALA TechSource blog. Harris, author of the *Infomancy Blog*, offers the following thoughts:

> The role of the school librarian in ten years will be to serve as a guide through the chaos of information . . . The library space will become more flexible, perhaps moving toward the idea of a university-like information commons with mainly digital nonfiction and reference collections, but still possessing high-quality fiction and picture-book sections . . . The school librarian will become more flexible—moving in and out of the library and classrooms as a curriculum and instructional pedagogy-consultant teacher. As education works to meet the needs of the so-called '21st century learners,' school librarians will have a key role in supporting an increased demand for information literacy and knowledge management throughout the content areas (ALA TechSource 6).

While Harris is looking forward and focusing on the newer technologies, I believe that his comments have application in the current school library environment as well.

- We presently serve as guides for patrons through the chaos of information; we do this in-person, and we should do this with our library Web presence.
- We are moving to digital nonfiction and reference collections—first through our periodical databases and electronic reference suites, now through virtual reference sources and ebooks.
- We are called upon to be curriculum and instruction specialists—teachers, instructional partners, and information specialists; we do this in-person, and we should do this

with our library Web presence also.
- We must provide information literacy instruction for our teachers and our students, not only in a face-to-face environment but also through the school library Web page, which patrons will use when we are not physically present to teach and assist.
- We provide knowledge management through the content areas as we connect our resources to the curriculum and make them available online, where our students are.

What is the exact future of school libraries? I do not have a crystal ball, so I do not know. I do know, however, that our patrons are online, and that our libraries must be there as well. My challenge to you is to:

1. Construct a well-designed and functional Web page for your library.
2. Remember that the Web site is for your patrons, not for you.
3. Lobby to have your library page prominently displayed as a link from your school's homepage. This not only provides ready access, but also makes a powerful statement about the place of the library in the school.
4. Be sure that your library Web page provides that gateway to electronic information and that you are meeting the information needs of your patrons.
5. Set a goal that your library Web page will be *the* place that your patrons look first for information.

List of Sites Mentioned

Table 7.1

Site	URL
21st Century Literacies	<www.kn.pacbell.com/wired/21stcent/gradelevel.html>
4JNet Guidelines	<www.4j.lane.edu/4jnet/4jnetguidelines.html>
Alexandria	<www.goalexandria.com>
Alliance for Physical Education, Health, Recreation, and Dance	<www.aahperd.org>
American Council on the Teaching of Foreign Language	<www.actfl.org>
American Library Association's Online Resources for Parents and Children	<www.ala.org/ala/oif/iftoolkits/litoolkit/onlineresources.htm >
American Memory Project	<memory.loc.gov/ammem/>
Ann Arbor District Library Teen Blogs	<www.aadl.org/services/axis>
Association for Library Service to Children Resources	<www.ala.org/alsc/parents.links.html>
Athena Web Server	<www.sagebrushcorp.com/tech/athena.cfm>
BadgerLink	<www.badgerlink.net>
Bartleby.com	<www.bartleby.com>
Bartlett's Familiar Quotations	<www.bartleby.com/100/>
Ben's Guide to Government for Kids	<bensguide.gpo.gov/>
BestWebquests.com	<bestwebquests.com/>
Biography.com	<www.biography.com/>
Boolean Searching on the Internet	<library.albany.edu/internet/boolean.html>
Choosing Search Tools	<www.noodletools.com/debbie/literacies/information/5locate/adviceengine.html>
CIA World Fact Book	<www.cia.gov/cia/publications/factbook/>
Citation Style for Research Papers	<www.liunet.edu/cwis/cwp/library/workshop/citation.htm>
Council for Exceptional Children	<www.cec.sped.org>
Cynthia Leitich Smith's Children's and Young Adult Literature Resources	<www.cynthialeitichsmith.com/lit_resources/cyalr_index.html>
Dictionary.com	<dictionary.reference.com>
Digital Book Index	<www.digitalbookindex.org>
Discoverer WebFind	<www.proquestk12.com/pic/pdfs/webselectdatasheet.pdf>
EBSCO	<www.epnet.com>
Educator's Reference Desk	<www.eduref.org>

EduScapes: A Site for Life-Long Learners of All Ages	<www.eduscapes.com>
ELM	<elm4you.org>
Encyclopaedia Britannica	<www.eb.com>
Facts on File	<www.factsonfile.com>
Fair Use Guidelines for Educational Multimedia	<www.utsystem.edu/ogc/intellectualproperty/ccmcguid.htm>
Farmer's Almanac	<www.farmersalmanac.com>
FedStats	<www.fedstats.gov/>
Finding Information on the Internet: A Tutorial	<www.lib.berkeley.edu/TeachingLib/Guides/Internet/FindInfo.html>
Firstgov.gov	<firstgov.gov/>
Five Criteria for Evaluating Web Sites	<www.library.cornell.edu/olinuris/ref/webcrit.html>
Fodor's	<www.fodors.com/>
Follett Library Resources	<www.flr.follett.com>
Follett One-Search	<www.fsc.follett.com/files/pdf/fiac_detail_10545a.pdf>
Follett Web Collection Plus	<www.fsc.follett.com/products/webcollection_plus/index.cfm>
Gale Junior Reference Collection	<www.gale.com/pdf/facts/jrcK12.pdf>
Gale Virtual Reference Library	<www.gale.com/gvrl>
GEM: Gateway to Educational Materials	<www.thegateway.org>
Georgia's Galileo	<www.Galileo.usg.edu>
Goochland County Public Schools	<www.glnd.k12.va.us/podcasts/blogs.shtml>
Greece Athena Media Center	<www.greece.k12.ny.us/ath/library/>
Greece Athena Media Center Virtual Reading Room	<www.greece.k12.ny.us/ath/library/reading_room/default.htm>
Greece Athena Media Research Guide (Big 6): Getting It Done—Six Steps to Success	<www.greece.k12.ny.us/ath/library/bigsix/default.htm>
Greenwood ebooks	<ebooks.greenwood.com>
Greenwood Electronic Media	<www.gem.greenwood.com>
Grolier	<go.grolier.com>
Guidelines for Implementing and Maintaining Virtual Reference Services	<www.ala.org/ala/rusa/rusaprotools/referenceguide/virtrefguidelines.htm>
Guidelines of Behavioral Performance of Reference and Information Service Providers	<www.ala.org/ala/rusa/rusaprotools/referenceguide/guidelinesbehavioral.htm>
H. W. Wilson	<www.hwwilson.com>
How to Cite Sources	<nb.wsd.wednet.edu/lmc/lmc_citingsources.htm>
How to Do Research	<www.kyvl.org/html/tutorial/research/>
ICYouSee: T is for Thinking: The ICYouSee Guide to Critical Thinking About What You See on the Web	<www.ithaca.edu/library/training/think.html>
IM A Librarian: Alexandrian Public Library	<www.apl.lib.in.us/im.html>
Indiana University's Clearinghouse on Reading, English, and Communication's Parent Link List	<reading.indiana.edu/www/indexfr.html>
Indiana's INSPIRE	<www.inspire.net>
Information Literacy and You	<www.libraries.psu.edu/instruction/infolit/andyou/infoyou.htm>
Information Please Almanac	<www.infoplease.com>
International Children's Digital Library	<www.childrenslibrary.org>
International Reading Association	<www.ira.org>
Internet Public Library	<www.ipl.org>
Jim Trelease on Reading	<www.trelease-on-reading.com/>

John Newbery Elementary School Library Media Center	<nb.wsd.wednet.edu/lmc/lmc_index.html>
John Newbery Elementary School Library Media Center Pathfinders for Grades K-5	<nb.wsd.wednet.edu/lmc/pathfinders/pathfinder.htm>
Joyce Kilmer Elementary School Media Center	<www.mahwah.k12.nj.us/jk/mediacenter/index.htm>
Kathy Schrock's Critical Evaluation of a Web Page Tool for Elementary, Middle, and High Schools	<school.discovery.com/schrockguide/evalelem.html>, <school.discovery.com/schrockguide/evalmidd.html>, <school.discovery.com/schrockguide/evalhigh.html>
Kathy Schrock's Guide for Educators	<school.discovery.com/schrockguide>
Kentucky Virtual Library	<www.kyvl.org>
KidsClick! Worlds of Web Searching	<www.rcls.org/wows/>
KidsConnect Tools	<www.ala.org/ala/aasl/schlibrariesandyou/k12students/aaslkctools.htm>
Librarian's Index to the Internet	<www.lii.org>
Library of Congress Learning Page	<www.loc.gov/learn>
Library Research Service Impact Studies	<www.lrs.org/impact.asp>
Loogootee Elementary West Evaluation Rubrics for Web Sites	<www.siec.k12.in.us/%7Ewest/online/eval.htm>
MAGNOLIA	<library.msstate.edu/magnolia>
Mapquest	<www.mapquest.com>
Marco Polo	<www.marcopolosearch.org>
MARVEL!	<libraries.maine.edu/mainedatabases/>
Maryland AskUsNow	<www.askusnow.info/about/>
Medline Plus Health Information	<medlineplus.gov/>
Michigan Electronic Library Reference Desk: Biography	<web.mel.org/viewtopic.jsp?id=336&pathid=1133>
Middle School Pathfinders from Lakewood Public Library for Lakewood Public Schools	<www.lkwdpl.org/schools/midschl.htm>
NASA	<www.nasa.gov/home/index.html>
National Atlas of the United States	<www.nationalatlas.gov/>
National Center for Education Statistics	<nces.ed.gov/>
National Council for Social Studies	<www.ncss.org>
National Council of Teachers of English	<www.ncte.org>
National Council of Teachers of Mathematics	<www.nctm.org>
National Digital Science Library	<ndsl.org>
National Science Teacher's Association	<www.nsta.org>
Nauset Public Schools	<nausetschools.org/research/works2.htm>
NCWiseOwl	<www.ncwiseowl.org>
NetLibrary ebooks	<www.oclc.org/info/k12subjectsets>
Netrekker	<www.nettrekker.com>
Netscape Composer	<wp.netscape.com/communicator/composer/v4.0/index.html>
Nvu	<www.nvu.com>
Occupational Outlook Handbook	<stats.bls.gov/oco/home.htm>
OneLook Dictionaries	<www.onelook.com>
Online Lessons	<mciu.org/~spjvweb/jvles.html>
Online Search Techniques	<webster.gtcc.cc.nc.us/library/searchtechniques.html>
Oregon Libraries Network L-net Chat	<live.247ref.org/wcscgi/CDM.exe?SS_COMMAND=CUST_SUP&Category=OR_K_12&VIRTCATEGORY=OR_ORSCHOOLS>

OSLIS/Oregon School Library Information System Beyond Surfing	<www.oslis.k12.or.us/secondary/index.php?page=beyondSurfing>
OSLIS/Oregon School Library Information System Citation Maker for Elementary	<www.oslis.k12.or.us/elementary/index.php?page=citeSources>
OSLIS/Oregon School Library Information System Elementary	<www.oslis.k12.or.us/elementary/index.php>
OSLIS/Oregon School Library Information System Middle and High School	<www.oslis.k12.or.us/secondary/index.php>
OSLIS/Oregon School Library Information System Secondary Citing Sources	<www.oslis.k12.or.us/secondary/index.php?page=citeSources>
Paideia School Library	<www.paideiaschool.org/library/default.htm>
POTUS: Presidents of the United States	<ipl.si.umich.edu/div/potus/>
Project Gutenberg	<www.gutenberg.org>
ProQuest	<www.proquestk12.com>
Quanta Plus	<quanta.kdewebdev.org/>
QuestionPro	<www.questionpro.com>
QUICK: Quality Information Checklist	<www.quick.org.uk/menu.htm>
Rand McNally Travel Directions	<www.randmcnally.com/>
Reading Rants and Raves, BookBreak! Berkley High School Book Blog	<www.bookbreak.blogspot.com/>
Research Rocket	<www.kyvl.org/html/kids/portal.html>
Rochester City School Libraries Ask-A-Librarian, Rochester, NY	<rochestersls.rcsdk12.org/ask.htm>
SIRS	<www.proquestk12.com>
SIRSI SingleSearch	<www.sirsi.com/Solutions/Prodserv/Products/ibistro.html>
SKS WebSelect	<www.proquestk12.com/pic/pdfs/webselectdatasheet.pdf>
Spectrum Web Catalog	<www.sagebrushcorp.com/tech/spectrum_webcatalog.cfm>
Springfield Township High School Library	<mciu.org/~spjvweb/>
Springfield Township High School Library Pathfinders	<mciu.org/%7Espjvweb/pathmenu.html>
Statistical Abstract of the United States	<www.census.gov/statab/www/>
Style Guide for Research Project Documentation	<www.paideiaschool.org/library/research/styleguide.htm>
Style Manuals & Writing Guides	<www.calstatela.edu/library/styleman.htm>
Surpass Web Safari	<www.surpasssoftware.com/websafari-centriva.htm>
SurveyMonkey	<www.surveymonkey.com>
SVC Redwings Virtual Reference Service	<library.skagit.edu/FAQvrs.html>
TALON: Taking Libraries Online Tutorial	<www.library.umw.edu/talon/outline.html>
Thomas Dale High School School Library Media Center	<chesterfield.k12.va.us/Schools/Dale_HS/library/Virtlib/media.htm>
Thomson Gale	<www.gale.com>
Thomson Gale PowerSearch	<www.gale.com/Technical/>
TILT:Texas Information Literacy Tutorial	<tilt.lib.utsystem.edu>
TLC CarlWeb	<www.tlcdelivers.com/tlc/carlweb.asp>
TLC WebFeat	<www.tlcdelivers.com/tlc/partnerships.asp?tpId=27&#partners>
U.S. State Department—Country Profiles	<www.state.gov/r/pa/ei/bgn/>
United Nations Cartographic Section	<www.un.org/Depts/Cartographic/english/htmain.htm>

United States Gazetteer	<www.census.gov/cgi-bin/gazetteer>
Usability Guidelines for Designing Web sites for Children	<www.nngroup.com/reports/kids/>
Usability Guidelines for Designing Web sites for Teenagers	<www.nngroup.com/reports/teens/>
Virginia SOL Released Test Items	<www.doe.virginia.gov/VDOE/Assessment/releasedtests.html>
Virginia SOL Test Blueprints	<www.doe.virginia.gov/VDOE/Assessment/soltests/home.html>
Virginia Standards of Learning	<www.doe.virginia.gov/VDOE/Superintendent/Sols/home.shtml>
Virtual Reference Desk AskA+ Locator	<www.vrd.org/locator/subject.shtml
Walter Reed Middle School Library	<www.lausd.k12.ca.us/Reed_MS/Library/>
Walter Reed Middle School Library Research Process Overview	<www.lausd.k12.ca.us/Reed_MS/Library/research/research.html>
Web Feet	<www.gale.com/pdf/facts/WebFeetK12.pdf>
Web MARC	<www.sagebrushcorp.com/tech/webmarc.cfm>
WebQuest Portal	<www.webquest.org>>
World Almanac for Kids	<www.worldalmanacforkids.com/>
WorldBook	<www.worldbookonline.com>
YourDictionary.com	<www.yourdictionary.com>
Zoomerang	<www.zoomerang.com>

Works Cited

Abilock, Debbie. "Homepage: Focus on the User." *Knowledge Quest* 33.3 (2005): 6-7.
Accessibility Guidelines: SDGC Web Guidelines. 14 January 2006. <http://www.greenville.k12.sc.us/district/web/policy/access.htm>
ALA TechSource. *The Digitally Re-Shifted School Library: A Conversation with Christopher Harris.* 2006. 7 February 2006. <http://www.techsource.ala.org/blog/2006/02/the-digitally-re-shifted-school-library-a-conversation-with-christopher-harris.html>.
American Association of School Librarians and Association for Educational Communications and Technology. *Information Power: Building Partnerships for Learning.* Chicago: American Library Association, 1998.
American Library Association. Reference and User Services Association. *Guidelines for Behavioral Performance of Reference and Information Service Providers.* June 2004. 30 April 2006. <http://www.ala.org/ala/rusa/rusaprotools/referenceguide/guidelinesbehavioral.htm>.
—. *Guidelines for Implementing and Maintaining Virtual Reference Services.* June 2004. 30 April 2006. <http://www.ala.org/ala/rusa/rusaprotools/referenceguide/virtrefguidelines.htm>.
Ask A Librarian: Florida's Virtual Reference Service. 12 May 2006. <http://www.askalibrarian.org/aal.asp>.

Baumbach, Donna J. "The School Library Media Center Web Page: An Opportunity Too Good to Miss." *Knowledge Quest* 33.3 (2005): 8-12.

Bell, Mary Ann. "State-Funded Informational Databases: You May Lose Them Even If You Use Them." *Teacher Librarian* 32.3 (2005): 8-11.

Blowers, Helene and Robin Bryan. *Weaving a Library Web Site: A Guide to Developing Children's Web Sites.* Chicago: American Library Association, 2004.

Born to be Wired: The Role of New Media for a Digital Generation. 2003. 15 February 2005. <http://us.i1.yimg.com/us.yimg.com/i/promo/btbw_2003/btbw_execsum.pdf>.

Brewer, Sally and Peggy Milam. "SLJ's Technology Survey." *School Library Journal* 51.6 (2005): 49-53.

Chicago Public Schools. *Chicago Public Schools Policy Manual: Student Acceptable Use of the CPS Network.* 26 March 2003. 30 April 2006. <http://policy.cps.k12.il.us/documents/604.2.pdf>.

Clark, Juleigh Muirhead. "Analyzing E-Mail Reference Service in a Museum Library: The Experience of Colonial Williamsburg's John D. Rockefeller, Jr. Library." *Implementing Digital Reference Services: Setting Standards and Making It Real.* Ed. R. David Lankes et al. New York: Neal-Schuman, 2003.

Clyde, Laurel A. "School Library Web Sites: 1996-2002." *The Electronic Library* 22.2 (2004): 158-167.

The Digital Disconnect: The Widening Gap Between Internet Savvy Students and Their Schools. 14 August 2002. 24 March 2005. <http://www.pewinternet.org/PPF/r/67/report_display.asp>.

Dodge, Bernie. *WebQuest Portal.* 2006. 10 May 2006. <http:webquest.org>.

Evans, G. Edward. *Developing Library and Information Center Collections: Fourth Edition.* Westport: Libraries Unlimited, 1999. Greenwood eBooks. 28 April 2006. <http://ebooks.greenwood.com/reader.jsp?x=20009399&p=20&bc=ELU8320>.

Fifty Years of Supporting Children's Learning: A History of Public School Libraries and Federal Legislation from 1953 to 2000 (NCES 2005-311). U.S. Department of Education, National Center for Education Statistics. Washington, D.C.: U.S. Government Printing

Office, 2005. 29 December 2005. <http://nces.ed.gov/pubs2005/2005311.pdf>.

Five Criteria for Evaluating Web Pages. 1998. 5 May 2006. <http://www.library.cornell.edu/olinuris/ref/webcrit.html>.

Florida Virtual School. 2006. 12 May 2006. <http://www.flvs.net>.

Fredericksen, Linda, Joel Cummings, and Lara Ursin. "User Perceptions and Virtual Services." *The Virtual Reference Experience: Integrating Theory into Practice.* Ed. R. David Lankes et al. New York: Neal-Schuman, 2004.

Goochland County Public Schools. 2006. 30 April 2006. <http://www.glnd.va.k12.us>.

Herring, James E. *Internet Information Skills: A Guide for Teachers and School Librarians.* London: Facet Publishing, 2004.

Hirko, Buff and Mary Bucher Ross. *Virtual Reference Training: The Complete Guide to Providing Anytime Anywhere Answers.* Chicago: ALA, 2004.

IASL/Concord School Library Web Page Award: Selection Criteria. 9 March 2003. 5 May 2006. <http://www.iasl-slo.org/web_criteria.html>.

Internet Access in U.S. Public Schools and Classrooms: 1994-2002 (NCES 2004-011). U.S. Department of Education, National Center for Education Statistics. Washington, D.C.: U.S. Government Printing Office, 2003. 29 December 2005. <http://nces.ed.gov/pubs2004/2004011.pdf>.

Jaeger, John. "Comparing Online Library and 'Ask an Expert' Sites." *Implementing Digital Reference Services: Setting Standards and Making It Real.* Ed. R. David Lankes et al. New York: Neal-Schuman, 2003.

Kentucky Virtual High School. 2004. 12 May 2006. <http://www.kvhs.org>.

KidsClick! Worlds of Web Searching. 1999. 10 May 2006. <http://www.rcls.org/wows/>.

Lamb, Annette. *Information Architecture for the Web: Website Evaluation.* August 2005. 5 May 2006. <http://eduscapes.com/arch/arch7.html>.

Lance, Keith Curry, Marcia J. Rodney, and Christine Hamilton-Pennell. *How School Librarians Help Kids Achieve Standards: The Second*

Colorado Study. April 2000. 15 January 2006. <http://www.lrs.org/documents/lmcstudies/CO/execsumm.pdf>.

Lee Rainie's Internet Librarians Speech: Shifting Worlds. 24 October 2005. 29 December 2005. <http://www.pewinternet.org/ppt/Lee%20Rainie%2010%2024%2005%20Internet%20Librarian%20speech.pdf >.

Lipow, Anne Grodzins. *The Virtual Reference Librarian's Handbook.* New York: Neal-Schuman, 2003.

Lippincott, Joan K. "Net Generation Students and Libraries." *Educating the Net Generation.* Eds. Diana G. Oblinger and James L. Oblinger. 2005. 24 March 2005. <http://www.educause.edu/NetGenerationStudentsandLibraries/6067>.

Loertscher, David V. and Douglas Achterman. *Increasing Academic Achievement Through the Library Media Center: A Guide for Teachers.* San Jose, CA: HiWillow Research, 2003.

Logan, Deborah Kay and Cynthia Lee Beuselinck. *K-12 Web Pages: Planning & Publishing Excellent School Web Sites.* Worthington, OH: Linworth, 2002.

Louisiana Virtual School. n.d. 12 May 2006. <http://www.louisianavirtualschool.net/?faq#2>.

MARVEL! Maine's Virtual Library. n.d. 12 May 2006. <http://libraries.maine.edu/mainedatabases/about.htm>

Minkel, Walter. "Chat Room: Selling Information Literacy." *School Library Journal* 48.2 (2002): 37.

—. "Remaking Your Web Site in Seven Easy Steps." *School Library Journal* 48.5 (2002): 46-49.

Neif, Ron."Beloit College Releases the Beloit College Mindset List for the Class of 2009. 24 August 2005. 30 December 2005. <http://www.beloit.edu/~pubaff/releases/mindset_2009.htm>.

Nielsen, Jakob. *F-Shaped Pattern for Reading Web Content.* 17 April 2006. 10 May 2006. <http://www.useit.com/alertbox/reading_pattern.html>.

—. *Kid's Corner: Website Usability for Children.* April 2002. 6 May 2006. <http://www.useit.com/alertbox/20020414.html>.

—. *Usability of Websites for Teenagers.* January 2005. 31 January 2005. <http://www.useit.com/alertbox/20050131.html>.

Palmen, Virginia. "Re: Blackboard and the Library." E-mail to the author. 12 January 2006.

Pomerantz, Jeffrey. "A Repeated Survey Analysis of AskERIC User Survey Data, 1998-2002." *The Virtual Reference Experience: Integrating Theory into Practice.* Ed. R. David Lankes et al. New York: Neal-Schuman, 2004.

Reid, Calvin. "E-books Go to School." *Publishers Weekly* 252.22 (2005): 28-29.

Reitz, Joan M. *ODLIS: Online Dictionary for Library and Information Science.* 2005. 15 May 2006. <http://lu.com/odlis>

Schmidt, Aaron. "The Young and the Wireless." *School Library Journal* 51.10 (2005): 44-46.

School Libraries Work! Research Foundation Paper. Danbury, CT: Scholastic Library Publishing, 2006.

School Library Media Centers: Selected Results from the Education Longitudinal Study of 2002 (ELS:2002) (NCES 2005-302). U.S. Department of Education, National Center for Education Statistics. Washington, D.C.: U.S. Government Printing Office, 2004. 29 December 2005. <http://nces.ed.gov/pubs2005/2005302.pdf>.

Schrock, Kathy. *Kathy Schrock's Guide for Educators: Critical Evaluation Surveys and Resources.* 2006. 5 May 2006. <http://school.discovery.com/schrockguide/eval.html>.

Search Engine Users. 23 January 2005. 15 February 2005. <http://www.pewinternet.org/pdfs/PIP_Searchengine_users.pdf>.

Tapscott, Don. *Growing Up Digital: The Rise of the Net Generation.* New York: McGraw-Hill, 1998.

Teachers' Tools for the 21st Century: A Report on Teachers' Use of Technology (NCES 2000-102). U.S. Department of Education, National Center for Education Statistics. Washington, D.C.: U.S. Government Printing Office, 2000. 29 December 2005. <http://nces.ed.gov/pubs2000/2000102A.pdf>.

Teen Content Creators and Consumers. 2 November 2005. 29 December 2005. <http://www.pewinternet.org/pdfs/PIP_Teens_Content_Creation.pdf>.

Teens Forge Forward with the Internet and Other New Technologies. 25 July 2005. 3 August 2005. <http://www.pewinternet.org/PPF/r/109/press_release.asp>.

Teens, Technology, and School. August 2005. 29 December 2005. <http://www.pewinternet.org/pdfs/PIP_Internet_and_schools_05.pdf>

Todd, Ross J. *OELMA Student Learning Through Ohio School Libraries: A Summary of the Ohio Research Study.* 2004. 29 December 2005. <http://www.oelma.org/StudentLearning/documents/OELMAResearchStudy8page.pdf>.

Valenza, Joyce. *Interface Creep: Or Will They Use Our Sites When We're Not Looking?* Online posting. 4 January 2006. 12 January 2006. <http://joycevalenza.edublogs.org>.

—. *Teens and Virtual Libraries: The Improvements They Really Want to See.* Online posting. 30 December 2005. 12 January 2006. <http://joycevalenza.edublogs.org>.

Virginia Department of Education's Virtual Advanced Placement School. n.d. 12 May 2006. <http://www.doe.virginia.gov/VDOE/Technology/VAPS.html>.

Warlick, David. "Building Web Sites That Work for Your Media Center." *Knowledge Quest* 33.3 (2005): 13-15.

—. *Redefining Literacy in the 21st Century.* Worthington, OH: Linworth, 2004.

Weblog Uses at Hunterdon Central Policies and Procedures. 30 April 2006. <http://static.hcrhs.k12.nj.us/gems/centralISP/uses.doc>.

Williams, Teresa D., Bonnie J. Grimble, and Marilyn Irwin. "Teachers' Link to Electronic Resources in the Library Media Center: A Local Study of Awareness, Knowledge, and Influence." *School Library Media Research* 7 (2004) 6 January 2005. <http://www.ala.org/ala/aasl/aaslpubsandjournals/slmrb/slmrcontents/volume72004/williams.htm>.

Young Children's Access to Computers in the Home and at School in 1999 and 2000, (NCES 2003-036). U.S. Department of Education, National Center for Education Statistics. Washington, D.C.: U.S. Government Printing Office, 2003. 29 December 2005. <http://nces.ed.gov/pubs2003/2003036.pdf>.

Index

A
Abilock, Debbie 54, 86, 87, 89

B
Baumbach, Donna 66, 95
Beloit College Mindset List 14, 26
Blackboard 44, 45
Blog 24, 25, 50, 59, 70, 71, 78, 104, 107, 108, 110
Bobby 90, 91

C
Citation 13, 30, 50, 57–59, 67, 107, 110
Clyde, Laurel A. 94, 95
Collection development 66, 68
Copyright 57, 69, 70

E
Ebooks 11, 13, 28, 30, 34, 36–39, 43–45, 69, 100, 104, 108, 109

F
Federated searching 43, 45

H
Harris, Christopher 104

I
Information literacy 15, 19, 21, 50, 53, 54, 61, 66, 67, 103–105, 108, 110
Information Power: Building Partnerships for Learning 12, 27, 49, 50, 65, 66, 83, 93, 103
Instant messaging 24, 25, 50, 60, 70–73, 75, 80

K
Kuhlthau, Carol 21

L
Lance, Keith Curry 22, 66
Loertscher, David 15
Logan, Deborah 69, 85

M
Marketing 66, 75, 76
Milbury, Peter 11, 94

N

National Center for Education Statistics (NCES) 16, 18, 20, 21, 25, 42, 109

Needs analysis 66, 73, 79

Nielsen, Jakob 87–89

No Child Left Behind 18

P

Pathfinders 44, 50–52, 62, 63, 66, 109, 110

Pew Internet and American Life Project 15–19

R

Readability 40, 89, 92

Reading promotion 59, 61, 66

Research process 20, 47, 50, 55–57

RUSA (Reference and User Services Association) *Guidelines* 73, 74, 108

S

Search tools 19, 20, 36, 43, 50, 53–55, 62, 107

State virtual libraries 94, 96, 101

T

Todd, Ross 15, 21, 66

U

Usability 80, 81, 87–90, 92, 111

V

Valenza, Joyce 17, 25, 43, 52, 54, 63, 68, 78

Virtual reference service 50, 60, 61, 67, 71, 73–75, 77, 80, 81, 108, 110

Virtual schools 94, 102, 103

W

Warlick, David 14, 23, 87

Web design 79, 84–86, 90, 92

Web site evaluation 55, 56, 79–82, 109

WebQuests 46, 50, 52, 107, 111

www.ingramcontent.com/pod-product-compliance
Lightning Source LLC
Chambersburg PA
CBHW070630300426
44113CB00010B/1723